MW00626376

THE RIGHT KIND OF RICH

WHAT I LEARNED ON THE PATH FROM EXTREME POVERTY to MULTIMILLION DOLLAR BUSINESS SUCCESS

RON OSBORNE

WITH HEATHER GOETTER

The Right Kind of Rich
What I Learned on the Path from Extreme Poverty to
Multimillion Dollar Business Success
Ron Osborne © 2022

Hardcover ISBN: 978-1-61206-270-9
Softcover ISBN: 978-1-61206-271-6
eBook ISBN: 978-1-61206-272-3

To purchase this book at quantity discounts, contact Aloha Publishing at alohapublishing@gmail.com

Published by:

AlohaPublishing.com

Printed in the United States of America

CONTENTS

Introduction   7

1   Know Who You Don't Want to Be   11

2   You Don't Have to Become Your Past   27

3   Don't Be Afraid to Be Different From Everyone Around You   39

4   Be Intentional With Your Family   59

5   Relationships Are the Key to Business   73

6   Do What Is Best for the Customer   95

7   Be Content and Don't Always Say No, but Mostly Say No   105

8   Hold On in the Tough Times   113

9   Keep a Balanced Perspective About Growth and Blessings   121

Conclusion   129

Acknowledgments   153

About the Author   157

INTRODUCTION

Walking into the physical therapy rehab center, where my adult son was recovering from a ravishing disease that almost ended his life, took me back 50 years. The wallpaper and fake plants were different, but the smell of disinfectant, the sounds of machines beeping over muted voices, and the flickering fluorescent lights made me feel once again like a small boy who had almost lost his dad to a stroke.

Fifty years later, I was a totally different person. Gone was the scrawny boy with bleached blonde hair that would get buzzed off when it had grown too shaggy. Gone were the ragged clothes, threadbare even when my older brother had gotten them, and the shoes two sizes too big.

In that boy's place stood a man who had risen out of the extreme poverty of his family, neighborhood, and community to become a successful businessman, family man, and community leader. I was surrounded by a close-knit family, loyal employees, and a faithful church. I could find no similarities between that lost boy and the man walking down the hall to his oldest son's rehab room.

My life journey was not accidental nor fortuitous. I chose the paths I walked, even at an early age. I analyzed the examples around me and knew I could be different. I knew I could choose who I was and who I wasn't.

Don't get me wrong—I am still human and didn't always make good choices. I messed up in a lot of small ways. But the things that were important to me—reaching my goals; being the best husband, father, and boss I could be; and finding stable income to keep my family out of poverty—motivated me to make choices that supported those goals. I also saw how some adults and teenagers got into drugs and alcohol to help them cope with their lives, and I made sure that I stayed far away from those things. I worked hard to avoid anything that could pull me down into the poverty mindset.

Even though I still live in Idaho and am only 160 miles from my childhood home, it feels like another planet. So many life truths have led me further away from the mentality of poverty I was raised under. The truths about life that I learned through my experiences enabled me to get out, even as I watched my family and friends break under the weight of poverty and continue the poverty cycle for their kids.

The path from a boy growing up under poverty to creating and eventually selling my business for millions of dollars was filled with simple life lessons. You can be successful too—not just in business but in all areas of life—if you can understand those lessons that took me decades to learn. Those lessons clearly show that wealth is much more than money. Wealth is about having healthy perspectives, being generous, and creating great relationships in business, family, and community.

These principles changed my life and they can change yours. They are simple but profound, doable but hard, life altering but slow to take effect. They might take a million decisions, but all those decisions will lead to one place: reaching your potential. And reaching your potential is not just for you, but for everyone around you.

> **If you allow yourself the freedom to let go of limiting beliefs—the mentality of poverty—in all areas of your life, you will truly succeed.**

1

KNOW WHO YOU DON'T WANT TO BE

I like to call myself the "Hillbilly from Heyburn."

If you walked into my house when I was growing up, you would have entered a dated little living room with plank flooring, a worn-down rug, a potbelly woodstove used to heat the house, and one stained old couch that smelled like cigarettes and faced the black-and-white TV. Off the living room was the kitchen with three dingy wood cupboards, a chipped counter, an ancient, groaning refrigerator, and a wobbly table with four mismatched chairs and one bench. The boys' room off the living room consisted of one bed I shared with my two brothers, squeezed next to a crank laundry wringer, shelves filled with paint cans and broken tools, and a galvanized wash basin stored on a hook that served as a tub for us boys. My sister slept in my parents' room until she was 8 years old. Then they built a wall to section off a six-foot space of their room for her. It was just big enough to fit her twin bed and a lamp.

We had no bathroom or running water in our house until I was 8 years old. We had an outhouse that was about five yards from the backdoor. Those 15 feet were no big deal in the spring, summer, and fall. However in the winter, that distance might as well have been a mile. I remember not wanting to take the time to get my coat and boots on to go to the bathroom, so I would race across the yard in my skivvies, do my business as quickly as possible while shivering, and get back to the potbellied wood-stove—the only really warm place in our house.

My childhood home in Heyburn, Idaho

The backyard was the best part of our home. It wasn't much to speak of, with its weeds and bare patches of dirt, but it did contain a few pigs, chickens, a garden, and a well pump. From late spring to early autumn, we ate fresh vegetables from our garden and occasionally fruit traded with neighbors. We would slaughter and butcher a pig about twice a year. And whenever a chicken was fully grown, we would do the same.

Harvesting chickens was my favorite chore. My dad or my big brother would chop off the chicken's head. My younger brother and I would then chase the headless chicken down so we could hang it and pluck it before dinner.

My mom preserved as much of the garden produce as she could for winter. When we inevitably ran out, our diet consisted of meat. Occasionally our pig and chicken meat would run out as well. If that happened, we went out into the wilderness and found a deer. It never mattered much if it was hunting season or not. We needed to eat.

My parents bought flour, yeast, milk, sugar, and other staples when they could. However, there seemed to always be something we needed and couldn't afford.

Our clothes and shoes came from hand-me-downs. My parents never had much money—however, strangely enough, they could always afford cigarettes and beer.

Both of my parents' parents came from extreme poverty and most people I grew up with lived in poverty. People in my community tried to escape the reality of their lives with drinking, drugs, or other addictions. And those addictions spiraled them further into poverty.

Dysfunction and poverty led many people in my community down the wrong path, mentally, physically, and financially. Most of the kids on my street had two parents, but those parents were usually not around during the day. The dads would be out of town working wherever they could find work and the moms worked locally in full-time domestic or hospitality jobs. My family was the one that was different, and I knew it.

Though the picture I have painted is grim, it was what I was used to. **The people I grew up with couldn't get out of the poverty mindset and cycle**. Everyone in my family was just the same—except me.

My mom got pregnant with my older brother when she was 16 and my dad was 15. They got married soon after she found out, had my brother, and then had my sister a short year later. A few years after that, they had two more kids—me and my younger brother.

As you can imagine, my parents never had a very good marriage. Though they never screamed or shouted, when I walked into a room where they were, I could feel the tension of the spoken words that I had missed. Even as a young child, I knew something was wrong with their relationship.

Due to a serious infection as a child that wasn't treated by doctors, my dad had a heart problem. When I was 8 years old, he suffered a major stroke. The stroke left him unable to work, walk, or talk well. He had to relearn everything. He spent months at a rehabilitation center three hours away and eventually was able to come home so my mom could help him. He was home, but not himself.

The years after the stroke were especially hard. My dad could no longer work. My mom took odd jobs like housecleaning and watching children, but after my dad came home from the rehabilitation center, she was needed at home most of the day to help him. We were eventually able to get social security money for my dad, but it barely paid the bills. Hunger and cold were never very far away.

We did have an uncle nearby and an angel of a neighbor just down the street named Mrs. Blankenship. Mrs. Blankenship's house was one of the houses that my mom cleaned. Mrs. Blankenship would invite us to her warm, clean, and quiet home and give us snacks. She also invited us to a holiday dinner a couple times a year. Her house was a second home to me. Having those memories really helped me in my childhood.

It was during this time that my older brother got into drugs. My dad had been a drinking man, being a bartender and a logger, but from what I know, he had stayed away from drugs. Not so with my brother. He started hanging out with the wrong crowd and getting into trouble. I could see what was happening with my brother and I knew, even as a little boy, that it would lead nowhere good.

My older brother started planting marijuana in my mom's garden bed. She complained to me one time that these ugly plants kept growing in her garden, even though she kept pulling them up. I had to tell her what they were and that my brother had planted them. She was not happy.

Dealing With Loss

Three years after my dad's stroke, he suffered a major heart attack one night and passed away suddenly. I was awakened by my crying mom. We all sat up, scared and wondering what was going on. She told us in her shaky voice that our dad had died.

It wasn't a shock; he hadn't been healthy for as long as I could remember. But it was extremely scary for me, and of course for my mom and siblings. What would we do now?

One of my brothers started crying next to me in the bed. My mom sat down next to him, put her arm around him, and cried with him. We all sat on our bed for a little while longer until my mom had to answer someone's question out in the living room. My brothers and I got up quietly, dressed, and stepped out of our cold room to meet the frenzy of neighbors and strangers in our house.

My mom had the hardest job. In the midst of planning my dad's funeral, figuring out our finances, and dealing with her grief, she still had four young kids in her care. I did what I could to help, but at age 10, that wasn't much.

My father's funeral was the hardest memory I have of my childhood. I remember standing there and hearing people share about his life. During the service, my mom broke down sobbing—I had never seen her like that before. She had always been the strong do-what-needs-to-be-done parent. Even now, I think of the overwhelming grief and uncertainty that caused her to fall apart that day—losing Dad, the burden of supporting four kids, being a widow at 33 years old, and having been the strong one for so many years.

Another hard loss happened a few years later. I had a half great-uncle on my dad's side whom I considered my grandpa. His name was Ira James Taylor but we called him Uncle Ari. Uncle Ari was my favorite. He lived just down the street and I would stop by his house on my way to school to eat breakfast and just sit with him. I can still remember the smell of bacon and other things he cooked for me. Uncle Ari was always there when I needed him, coming to my sports games that Mom couldn't make, giving me his hard-learned wisdom, and chuckling at my little kid humor. He made sure we were taken care of and if he could afford it, he helped out. He even paid for us to get a phone line a few years after my dad passed away.

One day when I was away for the night, Uncle Ari came over to see the family because he wasn't feeling well. While he was in the bathroom, he had a heart attack and passed away at the age of 66. I came home the next day to the news that Uncle Ari, another man in my life I loved, had passed away. My family knew how much he had meant to me, and they were glad that I hadn't been home when it happened.

I was devastated. First my dad and then my acting grandpa were gone. I processed my grief as a young boy would: anger, sadness, and then eventually resignation. Life was hard.

Both funerals, for my dad and Uncle Ari, were traumatizing for me. At my dad's funeral, I remember wearing very uncomfortable, stiff, itchy clothes. The shoes hurt my feet and the tie made me feel like I was choking. The funeral home where it was held was cold, dark, and smelled funny. During the service, I could see him lying in his casket looking like he was sleeping, but I knew he was gone. My heart ached with sadness and despair. After the service, I walked up to the casket and looked at him lying there, so still and silent. He obviously was not there anymore. It shook me to my core. My father was gone.

My uncle's funeral was similar. Both events left me feeling alone. To this day, I have a hard time attending funerals and when I do, I never go to the viewing.

After my dad died, my mom needed to get a full-time job. She hadn't finished high school, but she found a program that would train her to become a licensed practical nurse. She borrowed the money needed for the fee and studied and worked hard to become a nurse. I remember coming home from school and eating cold sandwiches and pickles that she had prepared quickly because she had to study. Thankfully, she passed the exam with flying colors and got a job at the local hospital where she worked for over 30 years.

This job brought money in, but now because my mother was working, income was still limited due to the minor social security benefits and low-wage jobs in our area. We were in the same state financially, still relying on pigs, chickens, and hunted deer for our main food source. But now, my three siblings and I were unsupervised from 7 a.m. to 5 p.m., six days a week.

It was during this time that every few weeks, my Uncle Ari would pick up me, my mom, and my brother in his pickup truck. We would head off to the local dump with us boys bouncing along in the bed of the truck. The next hour or so was spent moving trash bags and looking under big pieces of broken household items that people had dumped for anything useful we needed. We found garden tools, buckets, and the occasional chair or stool that we could use. We didn't find many treasures but we did find useful things that my mom or Uncle Ari could clean, fix, or repurpose.

Looking back, I realize that for my mom, the school year schedule was hard. She would wake us up as she was leaving for work. We got ready, ate breakfast, and headed to school. After school, we hung out with friends and came home about the time our mom got back from work, exhausted and ready to crash. She would whip up something for dinner, though sometimes she was too tired and we would find something to eat for ourselves by rummaging through the cupboards, and then we all went to bed.

It was during these years that my little brother started down the same path as my older brother, but at a much younger age. He and his friends started getting in trouble with the police in Heyburn. One evening a policeman brought him home after Mom had gotten back from work. He had been caught shoplifting during school hours, but they kept him at the station until my mom came home. She was so embarrassed. He was 13 at the time.

My brother kept getting in trouble, at school and with the police. Just a few months after his 14th birthday, he was caught selling drugs to some older kids. My mom was devastated. She skipped work to go to the hearing where the judge sentenced him to juvenile detention. It was both a sadness and a relief to my mom.

Most of the kids in my neighborhood were latchkey kids. Their parents worked constantly to survive financially. Those with two parents were still usually on their own a lot, because both parents worked outside the home. This situation was common and normal for me and those I knew, until I made a different type of friend with a more functional family years later.

Three Types of Learners

I have noticed that there are three types of learners in the world:

1. People who never learn

2. People who have to learn their lessons the hard way

3. People who can learn what not to do from others

My brothers were the first type. They both got into trouble and drugs at an early age and never got out. My sister was the second type. She made bad choices when it came to men she was involved with, and she really tried to get out of the pit she had dug for herself.

As you might guess, I am the third type. I watched what happened with my family, friends, classmates, and community, and knew that there was a different way. I wanted to make better choices. I didn't want my future wife (whoever she might be) to deal with the things that my mom had to deal with throughout her life.

Me (on the right), my mom, my youngest brother,
and my sister with Uncle Ari.

I knew who I didn't want to be. I remember clearly one of the first choices I made about who I didn't want to be. I had a fun group of friends in the 8th grade. We were all hanging out one day in the back parking lot of the one hotel in town. We weren't causing trouble, just talking, joking, and generally having fun.

Next, something happened that I would always remember. One of the kids produced a joint. He lit it and started passing it around like it was no big deal. I knew right then and there that I didn't want to be that person. I didn't want to be the guy who smoked weed with his friends. I didn't want to be the friend who went along and did what everybody else did.

I passed when it came to my turn and decided that I would find myself a new group of friends.

Hard Work Doesn't Have to Be Scary

Another choice I made early in my life involved getting a job, which also put me in the company of people with values and character. Though, not every work environment has these qualities.

I had a bit of experience working with my cousin for my uncle, cutting logs in the mountains. I loved the hard work and making an honest dollar (which was the amount we made by working hard from sunup to sundown each day). My uncle even treated us by paying for us to see a movie and get a soda at the end of the workweek.

The one summer I did that was transformative for me, though I didn't know it at the time. My uncle's family lived in a small camping trailer in the mountains for the summer, to be closer to work. My cousin and I slept in hammocks strung between trees near the camper. We would get up at the crack of dawn, eat a hot, delicious breakfast that my aunt cooked, climb into my uncle's big truck, and drive up a narrow dirt road to the mountainside of felled trees we needed to measure and cut.

> # It was the first time I learned
> # that hard work pays off.

That summer, I learned that I was not a guy who would try to get out of working hard.

My first year-round job was at a grocery store that was a bit shady. I got out of there as soon as I could and found a job working after school and weekends at Hudson Shoe Store. It was a good opportunity to work hard, dress well, become presentable, and learn customer service. I looked forward to working at Hudson's because it was a different environment than I was used to, and I enjoyed feeling like I could make something good of myself.

Jim Rohn, a motivational speaker, once said, "You're the average of the five people you spend the most time with." Now, as I look back at my life, I realize how true that is.

I am so grateful that even back then, I chose friends, mentors, and bosses whose examples helped me improve my character.

I worked with a man named Dick Wuthrich, who was the manager of the shoe store. Dick was my first real mentor. He talked to me about the future, about who I could become. He encouraged me to do my best in school, be honest, and work hard.

Dick taught me how to treat customers, how to present myself well, how to understand what the customer wanted and needed, how to talk respectably, and basically how not to be a hillbilly. I learned so much from that job. It was more than just selling shoes for me. It taught me about other types of people, and I quickly got comfortable around the class of people that could afford shoes from a shoe store.

That summer we would fish occasionally and fry up what we caught for dinner.

It was at this job that I got my first and second vehicles. My first vehicle was a 1958 Chevy truck that nickeled-and-dimed me with repairs. I knew it wouldn't last very long, so as soon as I could, I sold it (practically gave it away) and bought myself a 1959 Volkswagen Bug. I loved that car, and its only real issue was the lack of a working heater—and winter in southern Idaho can get colder than a polar bear's toenails. During the winter, my breath would condense on the windshield while I drove, and I had to scrape the *inside* of the windshield.

I bought that car when I was 15 years old. Having a car as a teen in my community was a big deal. People could see I was making different choices and living my life differently. Owning a car meant something different back then than it might mean today. It meant that you had a job, could save money, be responsible to pay for gas and insurance, and most likely had good grades.

Good grades came easy to me, though I wasn't afraid to work hard at school if needed. I started school in 1st grade (there were no public kindergartens back then) and I didn't know anything. No one read to me at home and I was never taught anything on purpose, though I did know how to count to 10 and some colorful vocabulary. On my first day of school, they tested us to see how well we could read. As you could guess, I was put in the lowest reading group. I began learning my letters and sounds, started putting those sounds together into words, and those words into sentences. I learned so quickly that within just a few weeks, I had moved up to the top reading group. And that is where I stayed for 12 years.

I loved all sorts of learning—not just reading, but math, science, geography, and history. I loved to be challenged in school and I usually had good relationships with the teachers and other students. I helped other kids with writing or spelling when I could and sometimes the teachers asked me to help other kids with math, which was the subject I excelled in the most.

School was more than just a place to excel and learn—it was the place that gave me stability and the opportunity not just to learn new things, but to learn from good people. Through my school years I had many impactful teachers and coaches. I remember how Mrs. Rasmussen, my 4th-grade teacher, responded to me when I returned to school after losing my dad. She showed genuine concern and compassion and to this day, when I remember her compassion, I get a bit choked up.

Another adult who made a huge impact on me was Terry Johnson. He was one of my teachers and my coach in 9th grade. He taught math class, which I loved, and I just bonded with him. At that point in my life, I didn't have many adult men I could look up to besides my boss at the shoe store. I was glad to find out he was going to teach at the high school the following year, where I had him for more classes.

Due to my family background, I had never thought about college and couldn't have afforded it even if I wanted to go. In fact, not many in my family had even graduated from high school. But my counselor in high school changed that for me. Her name was Ann Matthews, and I am eternally grateful for her. She challenged me to go to college. She helped me apply to my college of choice and helped me fill out forms for tuition aid as well as apply for scholarships and grants.

To me, attending college was this huge mountain that I couldn't even think about climbing, but she gave me the tools to conquer it. We spent many hours in her office, planning my next steps. She knew so much and shared with me everything she could. She was so encouraging and while listening to her, I started to feel like I might be able to succeed. My memories of her remind me to spend those extra moments with young people who might feel the same way I did at this time in my life.

2

YOU DON'T HAVE TO BECOME YOUR PAST

It is not easy to break free from poverty and the poverty mindset. I saw it all around me and grew up thinking it was normal, though I knew from an early age that it was not good. I also recognized by what I saw at school that my family was poorer than most. I wanted to be different.

There is one thing I did that helped me get out. It was not little or easy. It was met with resistance and misunderstanding, but it was important enough to me that I persisted. It turned out to be the key that set me on a path out of poverty.

That key is this: I made different choices.

Deliberate Choices

I looked at the example of my family and friends and decided that if I wanted to end up at a different place, I needed to choose a different path.

Those choices changed my life in many ways: I chose different friends, instead of ones who would lead me to drugs or having a kid in my teens. I worked hard at a job, not just coasting my way through work and quitting when I had money to spend. I dressed differently, knowing that how I felt about myself would reflect on how others felt about me. I set goals. I worked hard at those goals and even gave up sports and other fun activities to pursue those goals.

Years later, this same principle helped me succeed where others failed. It helped me grow a successful, thriving business. I made different choices.

The good, non-druggy friends I chose in school turned out to be kids from the Church of Jesus Christ of Latter-Day Saints. They came from good, stable families who attended the local LDS church. In high school, I started attending church with them and really enjoyed the community, fellowship, and structure. There were rules, but those rules were to keep people healthy and stable.

I enjoyed the community, teachings, and structure so much that when I began attending Minico High School, I joined seminary. For one class each school day, we walked over to the local LDS seminary and attended teachings. I loved it so much that I became the president of the local seminary my senior year. I helped organize youth events, lead group discussions, and travel to different Wards to share my story. Due to these opportunities, I realized that I loved being a leader.

It was early in my junior year that our seminary teacher encouraged us to plan on going on a two-year mission, once we turned 19. It piqued my interest and I spent weeks asking him all sorts of questions: What would we be doing? Where would I go? How would I get trained? How would I get there? How long would it be? His mission had been a life-changing experience for him, and I wanted the same thing. I thought about it and decided that was what I wanted to do.

I appreciated structure as a child. I think that was one of the reasons I loved school. It was stable and predictable. I knew that school wouldn't last forever so I had thought about joining the Air Force after I graduated to give me the stability and structure I craved. It would also help to get me out of Heyburn. *I was desperate to get out.*

But now I was presented with another option—going on a mission.

Setting a Goal

As I looked into how I could go on a mission, I learned I would have to pay for it myself. The amount of money I would potentially need was staggering to me. I almost decided I would never be able to go, but the more I thought about it, the more I wanted to do it. A few former missionaries shared with us about their experiences living in a foreign country, learning another language, and sharing and teaching. Determined to go, I decided not to let a little thing like money stop me.

Even though I was motivated to go, I was discouraged in the beginning. I knew I wouldn't receive any financial help from my family. My mom was just barely squeezing by and nobody else I knew ever had enough money, let alone extra money for anything besides surviving day to day.

By the beginning of my junior year of high school, I decided I wanted to go on a mission badly enough that I would do anything and everything I could to make it happen.

One of the things I loved to do was play sports. I had been on a baseball team since I was in elementary school and loved playing football in junior high and high school. I was a natural quarterback in junior high and excelled quickly in each sport I played. In high school, I played wide receiver on the football team and ran track my sophomore year.

I was a wide receiver my freshman and sophomore year (that's me with the ball, #31).

Despite loving sports and being around the students who also played sports, I was determined to do anything I could to fulfill the goal of going on a mission. I exchanged sports for work in my last two years of school, and it was a huge sacrifice. I missed my teammates, pushing myself to improve physically, and the challenge of competition. However, going on my mission was so important that I gave up every sport and requested to work in the shoe store as often as they needed me so I could to earn the money to pay for my mission.

I worked every afternoon and evening, Monday through Friday. I would come home from my job and do my homework and go to bed. On the weekends, I worked on Saturday, went to church on Sunday, and then began the school and workweek all over again.

Meeting a Girl

My schedule was hard. Occasionally I wanted to give up, but then I would think about getting out and seeing other places and making a difference. I stuck with that work and school schedule for over two years, slowly saving as much of my paycheck as possible. I didn't know exactly how much I needed, but I saved everything I could. Don't misunderstand me—I was still a teenager. I occasionally went bowling, hung out with my friends, or took a girl on a date.

In fact, there was one girl with long legs and red hair . . .

The first time I saw her was at a track meet when I was in 9th grade. I spotted her the moment I arrived. She was a cheerleader in a group of other cheerleaders, laughing and enjoying themselves. She was beautiful and I desperately wanted a chance to talk to her. The moment came when she was getting ready to cheer at the finish line. I passed her right after I finished my race and called out, "Nice legs, Red." She blushed the color of her hair.

Now don't get me wrong. I didn't get a chance to "talk" to her, but that interaction made her notice me. And that was enough for a 15-year-old kid. After asking around a bit, I found out her name was Carla. She had four siblings and lived on a farm just outside of Burley.

When I knew she would be at joint school events, I made it a point to show up. We eventually started talking and her friends helped me a great deal. They would drive her by where I was working and, with elbows and whispers, convince her to talk to me.

In the early spring of 1976, after I had turned 16 and just days before she turned 16, I called her and asked her if I could take her out for a date on her birthday. She had chosen not to date until she turned 16, and I wanted to be her first date.

She said yes.

I didn't want this to be just any date—I wanted to make a great impression. Since it was her birthday, I wanted it to be a big splash, too, and I thought it would be a good idea to include family and friends. I decided I was going to throw a "party." Grizzly Bear Pizza was the cool place to go for special occasions or even just for a nicer family dinner in Burley, Idaho. When I talked to Carla's mom about my idea, she told me this was Carla's favorite place and so we arranged for a private room. Her friends helped keep it a surprise.

My Volkswagen Bug and I picked her up at her house the evening of her birthday. She came out of her house dressed in a pretty blue skirt and white blouse. Her hair was braided into one single long red braid, which bounced with excitement as she climbed into my recently cleaned car. I played it cool, pretending like it was just going to be us two going to dinner and a movie. I even tried to throw her off the trail by asking her what movie she would like to see.

As we pulled into the parking lot, I hoped she wouldn't recognize any of her friends' or family's cars. Thankfully, she didn't. I held the restaurant door open for her, followed her into the bright, cheerful main room where Elton John was playing on the jukebox, and then without stopping, led her straight back through the regular tables to the party room. She was confused for a moment, but then her parents, siblings, and friends all yelled, "Happy birthday!" at the same time. The huge smile on her face made the work of planning everything worth it.

Throughout our lives, Carla has talked about the impact of that surprise 16th birthday party—almost as much as the giant life-sized Snoopy I bought her the following Christmas. That Snoopy was seriously beyond my budget but well worth it.

That birthday began our "going out" regularly. We eventually did have our first real date—just the two of us. We would go to dinner or grab a hamburger and milkshake at the local drive-in and just talk. I really enjoyed hearing her talk about her family, farm, animals, and school. All the adventures she loved made me want a different life even more. What would it be like to want to hang out with your family, be happy working with animals on your very own farm, or have the time for outdoor adventures? She inspired me to live differently with her zest for life.

She was my kind of girl.

Carla and I at her school dance our junior year.

We dated off and on for the next two years. As I got to know her family during this time, I found them to be nice and polite. My experience with girls' families was sadly lacking so I had no comparison. Much later I found out they didn't like me . . . at all—everyone except Carla's mom. They thought I was arrogant. It still boggles my mind. As I think back, I realize it might have been because I acted confident and self-assured. They saw a tall, thin, blonde kid with a quick smile and long hair. My facial hair also made me feel older.

I wasn't confident deep down. But I think I was compensating for coming from a hard place with a hard family life. That was how I overcame the poverty mindset that I grew up under. I overcompensated with confidence—extreme confidence.

One of the turning points that really impacted me and changed the way I would perceive family life throughout the rest of my life was when I went on a Sunday outing with Carla's family to Shoshone Falls near Twin Falls, Idaho. It was about an hour's drive, and for one of the first times in my life, I saw what a real family was supposed to be like. Her parents and each of her siblings genuinely cared about each other, and they showed it in the ways they talked to each other, listened, and respected one another, as well as enjoyed laughing and playing games. This was the life I wanted.

Not having experienced a healthy family growing up made me insecure around small children. My experience around kids had been extremely limited, and I didn't know how I should talk to or treat them. Because of this insecurity, I didn't interact with any children I came into contact with, including Carla's nieces and nephews. I think that was another reason they thought I was arrogant.

Those who know me now would never believe that I didn't like kids at any point in my life. Now, children are my favorite human beings on earth.

Carla's sister, at one point, told her that if Carla ended up marrying me, she would not come to the reception. I am thankful that my actions and attitude did not deter Carla one bit. She liked me. I liked her. We liked how we were together.

When we talked about that time years later, I was surprised by her perspective. She loved my confidence. She thought I was like no one else she knew. None of the other boys in her school or church had a job, owned a car so young, or grew facial hair. She knew I was going somewhere in life and that I would make something of myself. She also loved the fact that I was a gentleman and treated her well. She was extra impressed one time when I took her to a fancy restaurant and explained all of the knives and forks, though looking back, I wonder how I knew all of that dining etiquette.

Carla liked me despite my background as well. In fact, I made it a point to never bring her home to my house. I didn't want her to see my house, my brothers, or my neighborhood. Yet during Christmas break in 1977, she and her younger sister knocked on my door unannounced to bring me a Christmas present. I was so embarrassed as I answered the door, but being a gentleman, I invited them in and offered them something to drink.

As we sat in my tiny, dirty, smelly living room and talked, Carla seemed very comfortable, though I could tell that her sister was as nervous as I was. Would this change the way Carla treated me?

Spoiler alert: It didn't. In fact, years later she told me that visit made her admire me even more. She saw for herself what I had overcome. She was impressed that I was who I was even though I had come from such a hard place.

We found out over the years that our paths had crossed many times and we didn't know it. One of the first times was when I was 11 or 12 years old. My family would sign up to clean the rodeo stands between performances when the rodeo came to town. We worked hard cleaning up the spilled drinks, tobacco spit, snack wrappers, and dirt from so many boots. We emptied trash cans and cleaned bathrooms. While galloping her horse in the arena for 4H between performances when the stands were empty, Carla looked around her. She remembers seeing blonde kids about her age cleaning up. She says she remembers feeling an empathy and a connection to anyone who would have to do such "grimy work" when she didn't have to worry about working in that way for money at that age.

To her eye, those kids were obviously poor. She felt so bad for them. Her parents had taught her to have compassion for those who didn't grow up with the same advantages she had.

Those kids were my brothers and me. I was one of those grubby kids cleaning up after the people who could afford to go to the rodeo. We have talked many times over the years about all the places that our paths crossed—and it's clear we were supposed to meet.

Even though I grew up in the proverbial rodeo bleachers, cleaning up the trash of families better off than my own, my childhood and early teen years were spent with the desire to do something different—be someone different. Looking back, I can see now all of the small ways that I faced away from the path of poverty I had been born to walk. However, when I was experiencing life every day during that time, I couldn't see it. I didn't have the foresight—the eyes or mind to understand what I was choosing. And the choices were all so small. I didn't know if they would add up to make a difference.

If I had known what was coming; the huge choices I was about to make that would take me to a whole new world—an entirely different community and mindset—I might have had a different perspective. I might have been excited, or at the very least encouraged. But at that time, I had no guarantee that my path would end up anywhere except stuck on the north side of the Snake River in the Podunk town of Heyburn, Idaho.

3

DON'T BE AFRAID TO BE DIFFERENT FROM EVERYONE AROUND YOU

My senior year of high school began in the fall of 1977 and because I had accumulated enough credits, I only had to be at school for half days. The other half day was spent working at Hudson Shoe Store while continuing to save every penny for my mission. I was pretty good at selling shoes even though it was hourly and not commission.

With the encouragement and support of my high school counselor, I applied to attend Brigham Young University, an amazing LDS university in Provo, Utah. I didn't know what to think when I sent off my application. No one in my family had ever gone to college. It wasn't something anyone wanted or thought to do. It was daunting.

As I was waiting for the reply, I tried not to think about it. I focused on my last few classes and my work. I tried not to be nervous or fearful. Being denied would not be the end of my dreams.

Many weeks passed as I anxiously waited to hear if I was accepted, but one day after school I received a fat envelope in the mail from BYU. I had been accepted, and not only that, but I had been given a full tuition scholarship for the first year. This was the key to me being able to attend. That scholarship made it possible. I was astounded and relieved.

I was so happy to be graduating from high school.

As soon as I found out, I told my mom the good news. "Mom, I'm going to college and I'm never coming back." She understood. She knew I would never be happy living in Heyburn, Idaho.

College, here I come. To say that I was excited, nervous, and scared would be an understatement.

As I mentioned earlier, no one I was close to had ever gone to college. Yes, a couple of my friends (the ones from stable families) were planning on going, but they hadn't yet. I had only one person I could ask endless questions: my high school guidance counselor, Ms. Matthews. She didn't know everything, but she helped me figure it out: how to move, where to go, how to sign up to live in the dorms, and what I should bring.

Moving to a New Life

This new and scary adventure filled me with trepidation and nervousness, but more than anything, excitement. I was determined to figure out how to do everything I needed to do, knowing that I was doing things differently than my family. I was getting out.

The hardest thing about leaving my hometown of Heyburn was leaving my mom. For the last few years, after my youngest brother had gotten in trouble for drugs and gone to juvenile detention, it had just been the two of us. When neither of us were working, we had hung out, talked, laughed, and been there for each other. And now she would be alone.

It took me some time to grapple with this. I felt guilty. But I also knew I couldn't stay. I was pulled in two directions. I wanted to be there for my mom and I wanted to be anywhere else. I am thankful that she made the decision easy. She was so excited for me and refused to let me fuss and fret about her. I knew she had been through hard things before and had made it. She reminded me that she had raised four kids basically on her own. She would be fine now.

It helped that she was talking about moving out of our little shack and into a different house a few streets away. I knew she would have an easier time if she didn't have to worry about the repairs, upkeep, and expenses that seemed to pile up because of our old house. A newer home seemed like a much better idea, though it was not much of an upgrade.

One morning in August of 1978, I packed two bags I had bought to hold my personal belongings. After they were loaded in my Volkswagen Bug, I hugged my mom goodbye and headed off on my new adventure.

Brigham Young University in Provo, Utah, was a four-hour drive away. The first glimpse of the campus had me in awe. The buildings were beautiful, the grass and trees greener than anything I had seen, and the campus was filled with smiling students. I stopped and asked directions from a student who looked like he had been there before. He directed me to the right building. I found my dorm, where I had a large room that I shared with a friend from high school. We had signed up to be roommates months earlier. I moved my meager belongings into the dresser, laid my blanket and pillow on the bed, and was done moving in.

My course load in the first semester was perfect. I thoroughly enjoyed my classes. I loved learning and being challenged. In fact, one of the first classes I had was a college freshman math class. After the first couple of classes and looking through the textbook, I realized that I knew everything they were going to teach me. I plucked up my courage after the third class to walk down the steps to the front of the room and talk to the professor about moving on to the next level. He was surprised to hear that I thought I could pass the class right then and there. He challenged me to take the CLEP (College-Level Examination Program) test and if I passed it, I would get credit for the class. I thought that was a great idea and took the CLEP exam that next week. I passed with flying colors.

The university had high standards and I really enjoyed meeting them. I especially enjoyed exploring the city. Provo, Utah, is filled with fascinating museums, hiking trails that lead to beautiful vistas, and fun things to do. It was everything that Heyburn, Idaho, was not. It was a cool town that was energizing to me. I loved Provo.

Almost as soon as I had settled in, I started planning my mission. I could go when I was 19 years old, which was four months away. I planned to attend BYU for one semester and then pause my college education for two years to do my mission. Most of the guys and some of the girls at BYU started their freshmen year and then paused that for two years and continued their studies when they returned. BYU was accommodating that way.

The New World of Texas

On January 4, 1979, I said goodbye to my mom and my friends after being home for Christmas break. The first month I spent at the Missionary Training Center in Provo. I knew prior to the start of my mission that I was assigned to an English-speaking mission in southern Texas. I was a tad disappointed that I wouldn't get the opportunity to learn another language but was excited to know where I would call home for the next two years. Little did I know that I would become fluent in a second language during that time.

After being trained for a month, I was officially ready to go to San Antonio, Texas. I know for many people Texas is not very far away, but for me it might as well have been on the other side of the world. My world was small. The farthest I had ever been away from Heyburn was eastern Oregon. Three sides of three states made up my world: southern Idaho, northern Utah, and eastern Oregon. Texas was a million miles away. As you could guess, I was excited.

This photo was taken soon after I arrived in Texas for my mission.

Flying to southern Texas that February was my first flight in an airplane. It was awesome. My seat was thankfully next to a window. I loved the feeling of being pushed back in my seat as the plane accelerated from the runway to the sky. The roar of the engines and the view, looking over the brown landscape of frozen Utah, began a love affair with flying that I still have today. Surprisingly, I wasn't nervous at all.

Upon arriving, I discovered that 85 percent of the people I would be talking to and working with at my first assigned area, just north of the Mexican border, mainly spoke Spanish. And I only spoke English—hillbilly English. However, I decided that I would learn Spanish if it took me the entire two years. I would do this mission with my whole heart.

Giving my whole heart during those two years changed me. I said yes to every opportunity, met every person and family that I could, and spent all my free time learning the language and culture. I quickly found that the people in southern Texas were my kind of people: warm, welcoming, generous, family oriented, and fun. They opened their hearts, lives, and families to me. I learned to love their hospitality, their children, and their generosity. The way I was treated was the opposite from how I grew up. I was welcomed with open arms, spoiled with their hospitality, and treated like family. And the most interesting thing was that most of these people didn't have much money. Honestly, from what I could tell, they had about as much money as my family had—very little. But they didn't have a poverty mindset and weren't stuck in a poverty cycle. They didn't fear not having enough.

They were kind, loving, and generous.

A few times I felt guilty about having dinner with these Mexican families. They would feed me and my companion while the kids waited their turn to eat, watching us from the other side of the little room. I tried not to eat too much, but that was a problem too because the beautiful mamas wanted me to eat until I was stuffed and almost waddling.

My fellow missionaries and I taught in Wards, knocked on doors, talked to families, and traveled around helping wherever we could. We had our fair share of rejection, stress, and mishaps. But for everyone who slammed the door in our faces, there was someone who invited us in, engaged us in discussion, and encouraged us.

Every few months, I was assigned to a new area in southern Texas with a new companion. We usually worked in pairs, but occasionally we had a third person join us. I loved every minute of it. I loved the guys I worked with, the leaders I worked for, the people from the churches I worked with, and the communities I got involved in. It was a life-changing time for me.

In my spare time *and* when I was engaging with the community, I worked on learning Spanish. I went to the library on my day off and read Spanish children's books or watched videos in Spanish. By the time I had been in Texas for six months, I spoke it well enough not to need a translator. I was teaching in churches in Spanish, talking to families in Spanish, and using it in day-to-day interactions. Not too long after that, I started translating for my fellow missionaries. I loved it. Speaking the language helped me connect with people. I learned that connecting with others in their first language endeared me in their hearts. In fact, most of the people I met and worked with thought I was from California. I was thin, tall, and naturally bleached blonde. They got a shock when a young blonde kid greeted them and talked to them in their language.

These people loved me and I loved them.

Reconnecting With the Redhead

As the two years wound down, I thought of returning home with both excitement and sadness. However, one thing happened that grew the excitement and lessened the sadness. About three months before leaving, I unexpectedly received a letter in the mail from a beautiful redhead.

Carla had been on my mind often those two years. We had lost touch and I worried that she would get married while I was gone. The letters I had exchanged with my mom while on my mission had not contained a hint about Carla. In truth, I knew that my mom's world would not have intersected with Carla's. I figured she was probably married by then—she was fun, adventurous, beautiful, kind, compassionate, and responsible. Only a fool wouldn't want to marry her.

Carla's first letter caught me up on the last two years of her life. She talked about her family, the farm, getting her two-year degree at Ricks College (BYU Idaho), working, performing in a musical production, and attending BYU in Provo. She had been busy—maybe even too busy to date. I read that letter over and over again, devouring everything about it. Her handwriting was beautiful, her greeting sweet but reserved, and the contents interesting (maybe just to me). I may or may not have carried that letter with me for the first week, pulling it out to read again about her life at college or how her family was doing. I replied as soon as I could, and that started an exchange of letters that sprouted hope in my heart. Now the flight home couldn't come fast enough.

After arriving back in Salt Lake City, I hopped on the bus and began the long journey back to Heyburn. The bus seemed to stop at every tiny town to wait for any possible new riders. It gave me a lot of time to think. I thought about my life for the last two years, what I wanted for my future, and what I didn't want to happen.

By the time I got off the bus to my mom's tired but smiling face in the wee hours of the morning, I had a tentative plan: get a few hours' sleep, hop in my car (hoping that it would still start after being parked at my mom's place for two years), drive to see and connect with Carla (hoping that the spark was still there for her like it was for me), and see where life went from there. I was going back to college, and I hoped when I went back, Carla and I would be planning for our future.

In the morning I encountered a hitch to my plan. While on my mission, my mom had given my car to my younger brother when he had gotten out of his latest stint at prison because he needed a job and transportation. So I asked my mom if I could borrow her car after she got home from work and resigned myself to waiting all day.

The drive to Carla's house that evening felt especially long. It felt like I passed all my old life in that one drive. As I drove over the river that separated Heyburn from Burley, I thought about how separate my life was now from my childhood. I was a different person. I had made different choices that led me down new paths. There was nothing sad about it. I had not been held back by fear or the unknown. My choices had changed me.

Carla must have heard my car coming up the road because she was waiting on her front porch for me. She looked different but the same. If it was even possible, she was more beautiful than when I had seen her two years before and she also was more confident. She was dressed better than her regular farm clothes. She wore Levi's jeans with a pretty V-neck sweater. It reminded me of when I picked her up for her 16th birthday surprise party almost five years earlier. But she was different in other ways too—she had grown up.

My stomach flipped a few times as I pulled to a stop, turned off the car on her driveway, and got out. Was this really happening? A ridiculous grin broke across my face. I walked over and wrapped my arms around her. I held on as long as I could, then reluctantly let her go. Stepping back, I said, "Hi."

She glowed.

Carla ushered me into the house to see her parents and sister. I greeted everyone, and parked myself in my favorite spot, next to the fireplace on the stone hearth. We talked and I answered her parents' questions about my mission and what it had been like. I also told them about my plans to go back to BYU and finish my degree. As we talked and caught up, I found my eyes wandering back to Carla over and over again. And every time I caught her looking at me, my stomach did a little flippity-flop. I wondered if Carla was feeling the same thing. By the pink tinge of her cheeks that would come and go every time she looked at me, I was hopeful.

Toward evening, Carla's brother, his wife, and their toddler arrived. Carla's niece toddled into the living room and stopped short when she saw me, a total stranger. I smiled at her and held out my arms to her to see if she would come sit with me.

I had spent two years with families, playing with and enjoying kids, and had discovered that I loved them—all ages and sizes. Carla's niece hesitated only a second and then ran across the living room and climbed up on my lap. I had been accepted.

Carla told me later that was the moment she and her whole family knew I had changed. They loved the new Ronnie Osborne.

We spent almost that entire Christmas holiday week and New Year together. I figured out a way to get a car (a friend of mine asked his dad to help me get a small loan for an old car) and also worked at my old Hudson Shoe Store job to make some cash so I could pay for gas and take Carla out.

I consider myself a romantic guy. For years after we were married (spoiler alert), I brought Carla flowers at least once a week. However, one day about two weeks after I had returned from Texas, we were driving somewhere and I looked over at her and said, "So are you going to marry me?" She didn't answer, but by the smile that broke out on her face, I knew that she would.

After my proposal (even though it was so lame), we started planning our life together. After we returned to BYU, we spent as much time together as was possible with our classes, work, and activities, though it wasn't enough for me. I wanted our life together to begin as soon as possible.

February was the month that I finally got a chance to talk to her father. We returned for a long weekend to visit our parents. We drove home on Friday after her last class, and I showed up bright and early Saturday morning and asked to speak to him about marrying his daughter. His response was, "What took you so long?"

Marrying Into a Real Family

The process of getting married was not quick or smooth. Carla had started traveling with her musical production when it was on the road. At first it was for long weekends around the college schedule, but as college wrapped up, the show started traveling more and more. She was the assistant director, an actress, and a dancer, and was also in charge of coordinating everything every time they moved to a new city, including the merchandise. In between all of this, she was planning our wedding and reception, which was turning out to be as big a production as her traveling show. I did what I could, but that was very little.

We decided to set the wedding date for when the production was on a break near the end of summer. We would get married, celebrate our honeymoon, and then Carla could go back to work and be on the road when needed.

Carla and I were married September 4, 1981, in the Logan Utah Temple. I was excited and nervous to be marrying her—excited because I couldn't believe that she would finally be mine and nervous because of the responsibility that having a wife and a family would bring.

The morning of the wedding dawned, and I was a wreck while getting ready. My stomach was in excited knots as I took a shower, got dressed, and gelled my hair. I forced myself to eat breakfast because I knew it would be a long day and I needed to start it right. I wondered how Carla would look with her red wavy hair hanging down her back. I didn't know what her dress would look like, but I knew she would be gorgeous.

Our wedding reception.

We had a small group of family to witness the sealing ceremony in the temple, mostly made up of her family and my mom, who had joined the church a couple years after me. I was so grateful that she could be there. The drive from the temple to Burley, Idaho, was two hours, so Carla's parents had arranged a small sit-down meal after the ceremony for those who attended. We changed into our reception clothes, me in a gray suit and Carla in her white dress. I stood up during the meal and made a short speech, though I couldn't tell you even one word that I said on that day. After that event, during which we ate very little because we were still too wound up, we loaded in cars and headed off to the reception in Burley.

The reception was a whole different story, with somewhere between 800 and 1,000 attending because of the tight community that Carla's family, the Cranes, had in and around Burley. My side was a bit smaller, made up of my mom, sister, an uncle, and my close friends. I didn't mind. I loved that I was marrying into a healthy, vibrant family with a supportive community.

Carla and I were able to greet everyone in the reception line before they found a table. I was dizzy with all the names, relations, and well-wishes by the time everyone had gone in to get their tables. One of the blessings of having a huge reception was the pile of wedding gifts that we received (four toasters!). We felt like we were set for life.

After our reception and honeymoon, we moved to Springville, Utah, and I settled into life while Carla came and went with the musical production.

Significant Connections

One of the connections I made in Texas on my mission was fairly insignificant at the time but would come to change my whole life. I met a bishop in the church. He was one of the senior executives of Amicable Insurance Company in Waco, Texas. This gentleman asked what my plans were when I left. I told him I planned on continuing my education at BYU and getting a job. He nodded and told me that Amicable Insurance had one of the most successful offices in Salt Lake City, run by a man named Darryl Nelson. He knew Darryl would be an amazing mentor for me. He asked me to look him up when I got back if I needed a job. He had confidence that I could excel in that field.

Soon after returning to BYU, I received a phone call from Darryl Nelson's assistant, asking if I could meet with him and talk about joining the team. We met and hit it off right away. I decided to give insurance a try. It was a decision that would change my life.

As a general rule, most insurance agents live on pure commissions, but this company had a program where they paid you an advance in the beginning so you could live while building up your commissions. They had me fill out a form to help me figure out what I needed to live on, moneywise. I was a new college student, fresh off a mission where I had been living on $175 a month for the last two years. I filled out the form and tried to make up everything I might need (and I do mean "make up"). The highest total I could come up with was $800 a month and even that was a stretch. It felt like a fortune!

I nervously brought the form in and sat down with Darryl. After greeting him and handing over the form, he quietly looked over everything while slowly shaking his head side to side. I got really worried. Did I write down too much? Am I coming across as greedy? After what felt like an hour but was probably about three minutes, he looked at me with a half-smile and said, "Let's put this total at $1,200, okay?"

Letting out the breath I didn't realize I had been holding, I thought, *Wow, 50 percent more than I could even make up!* I felt rich for the first time in my life.

Selling insurance fit me to a tee.

Selling individual life and disability insurance was challenging but I loved it. I loved meeting new people, helping them better their lives, meeting and exceeding goals, and the challenge of winning incentives like gifts and trips. Insurance fit me to a tee.

I was so successful right from the beginning that I started talking to Carla about pursuing insurance full time. My scholarship had ended at the end of my freshman year and I couldn't afford to continue college. And now I had a wife to support and an apartment and bills to pay. I had spent the last number of years not being afraid to be different from everyone and I approached this next step the same way. Should I get student loans and finish my education like everyone around me, or should I step out and do something different? I withdrew from BYU and focused 100 percent on my career.

By this time, the musical production was winding down and Carla knew she needed to be done. We wanted to start a family and be together without her having to be on the road regularly. She bade farewell to her production family and the crazy life of the stage and travel.

Our time in Utah was good. Learning a new career with all that entailed challenged me. It was a steep learning curve, but I loved every new thing I learned and every new person I met. Finding each client's needs, learning how to tailor their insurance to fill those needs, and connecting with them personally, not just professionally, kept me engaged and interested in my work. My clients became my friends.

Because of the natural connection I had with people and because of my drive to succeed in every area of my life, I was extremely successful. Back then, insurance companies offered vacation trips as an incentive for their top-producing agents. That incentive worked for me. I would find out what was required to qualify for them and aim to get there.

Within a few years after starting in insurance, Carla and I were going on trips completely paid for by the insurance companies. I remember the first trip I won. It was a huge thing for me—the kid who grew up with no vacations—and for Carla, whose family couldn't be away from the farm for more than a night. We won a cruise in the Caribbean. They gave us the smallest room in the bottom of the ship, but we didn't care. We were thrilled to be on a cruise and felt like a king and queen.

In the beginning we won one trip every year or so, but eventually we qualified for two in a year, and much later, we won three trips to Hawaii in one year. Even when children joined our family, we continued taking advantage of the trips.

For the first few years of our marriage, Carla worked full time. After finishing with the musical production, she worked as a substitute teacher and had other various jobs. Because I wanted her to be able to stay home with our kids when we had them, I made sure that we could live on my income alone. This enabled us to put everything Carla earned into a savings account, which gave us a head start on the down payment of our first house.

We started thinking about moving closer to Carla's parents and my mom. We loved our families and missed being close to them. I also realized that I would have a ready-made community that could expand my reach of clients while still serving my loyal current customers. I knew more people there and that would help get more customers.

Homecoming

I reconnected with Greg, a friend from Hudson Shoe Store who went to school with Carla. He had joined the LDS church about the same time I did as a teenager and ended up marrying a girl who had gone to school with me. His dad owned an insurance agency. I started my own agency and rented a little office from them. They were in the property casualty insurance business, and we would send each other leads if we had clients that had insurance needs outside of our specialty. It was fun working with a friend.

Carla and I moved into a tiny home we rented from her parents on their farm about five miles outside of Burley. Carla was so good at making it ours, decorating it and filling it with joy, comfort, and laughter. It was a small place, but we loved it. We decided soon after moving to Burley that we were both ready to grow our family.

Being back in the area, just a few miles from my childhood community, was surprisingly peaceful. I had expected to feel something besides excitement—something negative. But being who I was now, a totally different person with an amazing wife, a promising financial future, and the possibility of becoming a dad, kept me grounded and looking forward. I could foresee a few of the blessings that might come our way and I was excited for the future.

4

BE INTENTIONAL WITH YOUR FAMILY

Family means a lot to me now. Growing up, family was challenging. My mom was the only one who had been there for me, and I was the only one she could rely on. It had been the two of us through most of my childhood. When I joined Carla's family, family meant something else. I had friends, mentors, a partner in life, and kids everywhere. I loved it. And because of the life and joy that they brought, I was excited to have a big family of my own. I knew I wanted to teach them, play with them, read to them, take them on adventures, and snuggle down and cuddle with them. I wanted to be there for them.

AJ (Austin James) was the beginning of the fulfillment of that dream. Carla had significant health issues for a long time, and we considered AJ our miracle baby.

Soon after Carla had AJ and was still in the hospital, my mom, who worked at the hospital, started popping in every once in a while to make sure we were okay. On one of her first visits, she asked what we were going to name the baby. We told her,

"AJ." She froze for a second after hearing our choice and asked, "How do you spell that?" I told her, "A. J." She huffed a bit and very clearly told us that we could not name a child only initials—he had to have a real name.

Well that took us aback. We really only wanted to name him AJ. Not even questioning if my mom was right, we started discussing possible names that would work for AJ. Austin had been on our "name" list and so we zeroed in on that one first. Finally, after a bit of back and forth, we decided that *James* went really well with *Austin* and so AJ was named.

The day we brought AJ home from the hospital, the nurses loaded Carla into a wheelchair, placed AJ in her arms, and wheeled her to the curb where I was waiting with the car. After I helped her into the car, it hit me—AJ was ours. We were responsible to take care of him. The doctors and nurses didn't give us an owner's manual. How were we supposed to not only keep him alive, but raise him to be a good man? The responsibility was daunting.

The first few weeks of AJ's life were filled with joy, fear, insomnia, rocking, laughter, and crying. AJ cried a little bit too. We were so lucky to have family close and we got a lot of help—advice that helped to ease our many fears, and Carla's sisters showed up to help us take care of our precious baby boy.

And nearly as soon as AJ was rolling around, we found out that Carla was expecting again. As a new full-time mom, she was shocked and a bit overwhelmed at the thought, but I was in heaven. Two babies in one year!

Alivia Leigh was born on June 9, 13 months after AJ. Adjusting to two babies was challenging but fulfilling. If it was possible, Livi was even more beautiful than AJ.

Unfortunately, Carla was sick for a long time so I tried to help out as much as I could. I spent evenings and weekends connecting with clients who worked 9-5, so I would try and give Carla a break for a little while during the day to rest. She was a rock star. She was so deliberate about spending time with each of the babies separately. She took AJ out to go on little adventures looking for shiny rocks, strange bugs, or beautiful flowers. She rocked and read to Livi while AJ napped.

Me with AJ, Livi, Trevor, and Taylor in 1993.

We decided to wait a few years to have another. We wanted to focus on AJ and Livi and enjoy them, so it wasn't until four years later that Trevor Kade joined our family. By this time, AJ and Livi were beginning school, so Carla was ready to focus on another baby. This worked out so well, we decided four years later that we needed one more. Taylor Shea, named after my Uncle Ari (Ira James Taylor), completed our family. We were happy and done.

Purposeful Parenting

Because I hadn't had a good example as a father, I wanted to be the very best father I could possibly be. And thankfully, by the time the kids were out of the baby stage, I had shifted my business to be more work focused during the day, which left me with evenings and weekends to love on, spend time with, and teach and inspire my remarkable children.

One of the truths I quickly realized was that you can't parent by accident. Teaching, training, and building a relationship with your kids has to be on purpose. Choosing proactive and not reactive parenting has led to raising four amazing humans who work hard, dream big, and walk tall.

In the beginning when the kids were young, it was harder to be a proactive parent. The days were filled with diapers, feeding, yelling (from excitement or anger), naps, and play. We tried to establish a routine but also gave ourselves grace to just make it through some days. Carla was the best at parenting when the kids were little. I learned so much from her.

When they were little, I loved to get down and play, read books before bed, and go on backyard adventures with them. As they got a bit older, I got more deliberate about teaching them things like bike riding and other simple life skills. I also started leading the boys' Boy Scout groups.

One time I took Livi on a business trip when we lived in northern Idaho. She was about 5 or 6 years old, and we had fun driving together, getting junk food (because Mom wasn't around), and having rambling chats. While we were heading south, driving through a beautiful valley of lush grass, out of the blue Livi asked me in a serious voice, "Daddy, what's stock?"

I was flabbergasted. Where had she heard about stocks? Excited, I launched into a simple explanation about the stock market, investing for the future, buying low and selling high, and a few other details. After I was done, silence reigned for a minute. She finally looked over at me from her booster in the passenger seat and asked in her little high voice. "Then how do stocks cross the road?" I couldn't help but laugh out loud. She was asking about a sign we had just passed: Stock Crossing. Still chucking to myself, I explained to her what the other type of "stock" was. I laughed to myself for quite a while about that one.

I had many other fun and amusing situations happen when the kids were little but without a doubt, my favorite time was the teen and young adult years. All four kids were like sponges concerning almost anything I took the time to talk about with them. In fact, I loved talking about work, investments, people, culture, friends, learning, perseverance, character, and more complicated yet important subjects in life. While on our family trips, I brought business-related information along and spent time teaching and training the kids, as they showed interest.

AJ took his business notebook everywhere—even on vacation.

AJ was the one who showed the most interest in business. I have more than one photo of us as a family posing for the camera while out to eat or on vacation and he has his notebook, which contained business information he was learning from me, tucked under his arm. He soaked up every little bit of business information that I could teach him.

Alivia loved other cultures and after college ended up getting a job in New York City, working for the United Nations. She had a real desire to not only adventure around the world, but also to make a difference in the world. I was afraid she would never move home. Thankfully she eventually did and now she and her husband are happily settled in Idaho where we can see our grandkids regularly.

Trevor, like AJ, showed interest in business when he hit his teen years and I spent time teaching him. He also was passionate about getting involved with local politics. He was heavily involved in student government at his high school and served on Meridian, Idaho's Mayor's Youth Advisory Council during his junior and senior year.

Taylor was the complete opposite of his brothers. While growing up, he was laid back and always the peacemaker. He wasn't passionate about business or politics, but was fiercely patriotic, highly logical and organized, and loved all branches of the military. In fact, starting at a very young age, he and I used to watch *M.A.S.H.* every night. He is currently serving in the Army as a 1st lieutenant and we both find it funny how so many situations that he encounters are similar to our favorite old show, *M.A.S.H.*

Every one of our children had things they struggled with and things they excelled in. We worked through learning, physical, and emotional challenges, but as we faced each hardship and unknown head-on and together as a family, we became better parents and people.

Carla and I were deliberate with our family in other ways too. We wanted to always foster a good relationship with our kids, so we made sure not to overreact when they shared something shocking. Instead, we would react calmly but later talk to them about the wisdom and results of making good choices. If they still made wrong choices, we allowed (and sometimes created) the natural consequences that were sure to follow.

We also wanted our kids to have good work ethics. As a result of my successful business ventures, we usually had more than enough income to live on, but we never wanted to raise rich kids. In fact, there was a time when the younger boys were getting harassed for being "rich kids" and they were adamant that we were not "rich." It was not long after that I had to sit them down and let them know that yes, we were in fact very well off. We were doing so well that I was in the market to become partial owner of a private jet. They were shocked.

One of the ways we promoted learning to work hard was by sending them to work on Carla's family farm during the summers of their teen years. Carla's brother, Dennis, ran the farm, and he was more than happy to take them in, bunk them, and work them from sunup to sundown. These were transformative summers. They usually returned to us feeling satisfied with their hard work but also determined to become an expert in something other than farming.

We made sure to teach them that helping around the house was not, in fact, something they would get "paid" for. Daily and weekly chores in the house, outside, and with the horses were expected contributions to the family. We had a large house by the time Trevor and Taylor were teens, and Carla had acquired a few horses by then (which may or may not have been gifts from me). This kept the boys busy helping where needed.

As the kids grew closer to the friends-focused years, Carla and I wanted our home to be the hangout for the kids, teens, and young adults. We made sure that all the friends felt welcome, even the more challenging ones. We were deliberate about having fun toys: a pool, trampoline, swing set, basketball hoop, and bikes. We kept good snacks, sandwich makings, drinks, and treats stocked and in abundance. We also made it clear that everyone was welcome to help themselves without asking.

I remember one time we were arriving home from a family trip and we walked in the house and passed the kitchen. One of AJ's friends was in the kitchen making a sandwich. We greeted him and as I was walking upstairs to take my bag to my room, I thought, "That should be strange but really isn't." In my childhood, I had friends but I never wanted them in my home. I didn't want them to see the tiny, dirty living room, my bedroom that was more storage closet than room, our empty cupboards, or our lack of running water and bathroom. We would either play outside or at their house, especially once my dad had died and my mom was working full time as a nurse.

I was and am constantly amazed at how different life is for our family. I don't take it for granted and I wanted my kids to understand and appreciate what they had. As they were growing up, I not only talked about how I lived but also took them back to my old neighborhood occasionally and pointed out where those things happened.

Though Carla's upbringing was different than mine in all the good ways, we both were raised believing similar things: work hard, save your money, have compassion for others, and help when you see a need.

Our family in 2001.

We also wanted our children to understand who they were in relation to the rest of the world. Carla and I made sure that when we were on our family trips, the kids got to see parts of the real world they were visiting. We didn't stay in the resorts or on the cruise ships the whole time. We were deliberate about taking day trips to see the local people and how they lived. If possible, we would stop and eat in local restaurants and try to engage the locals in conversation and learn something about them. I have been grateful many times that I never lost the Spanish I learned while on my mission.

Years later when our kids were adults and had kids of their own, they would tell me how much those trips and that perspective had affected them. They thought at the time that our visiting the "real" world happened only because we enjoyed it. But I assure you, it was intentional. Like I mentioned earlier, neither Carla nor I wanted to raise "rich" kids. We wanted them to appreciate where they came from and understand what they had to be grateful for—a loving family, a secure future, and an opportunity to be whoever they wanted to be.

Maintaining Connections

One of the other ways we were intentional about raising our kids was occasionally asking each other if there was anything we needed to address or change in our lives. For years during the kids' elementary and teen years, about once a month I took turns sitting down with each of them separately and asking them how they were, any struggles they were dealing with, and if they had anything they wanted to ask me or wanted to know. It was amazing hearing from each of them and seeing the world from their perspectives. I had so many really good conversations about life, school, friends, goals, business, money, investments, culture, perspective, and a myriad of other subjects.

About the time AJ left on his mission at 19 years old, Carla and I realized that we needed to get rid of regular TV. Livi was in college at the time, so we only had Trevor and Taylor in the house. They would have been about 14 and 10 years old. We sat down with the boys one Sunday afternoon and started with, "Boys, we think we need to get rid of television." We explained our reasoning and gave them time to get on board. It took one of them a little longer than the other to finally agree, but when he eventually agreed and we removed it, our family life changed. As I look back now, it was one of the best things we did as a family. We started spending more time together and had more talks about all sorts of stuff, including business and life. We talked more, studied together, and spent so much more quality time together.

As our teens became young adults, we dealt with the normal growing-into-your-own-adult pains. But through all of the rough stuff, both Carla and I made sure to keep good relationships with our kids, hear their hearts even when we disagreed with them, and be their biggest advocates. We loved them, were proud of them, and wanted to be a safe place from the harshness of the world.

Each of our kids is very different from the others. Even as small children, their personalities shined. Carla and I found that in some ways we needed to respond to our children differently. Some were more sensitive than others and a raised voice would cause melting into tears. Some were louder (though our whole family was fairly loud overall) and more outgoing, and they didn't care about a raised voice, but being grounded was devastating. Each of our sons got involved in various things, including government at school and locally, with soccer and business. They were also involved in Boy Scouts and every one became an Eagle Scout. Livi loved school, other cultures, and adventures. But in character growth, we made sure to hold the same standards and rules for everybody (including the parents). We put family first and all that implied, we were all involved in church, and we contributed to the home and community.

Throughout our kids' growing-up years, I worked sunup to sundown. I made sure to be there for family dinners, sports games, church events, and growing milestones, but I credit so much of who our kids were and are to Carla. Marrying her was the number one smartest decision of my life. She was devoted to each of them and walked them through the day-to-day hard growing-up times and the fun kid stuff.

Looking back over the years, I learned that partnering with a healthy others-focused human being is an essential component to raising healthy others-focused kids. I still wake up every day thankful for my life partner, and I look for ways to let her know what she means to me. I know that sometimes we have to raise our kids without that marriage partner, but it is still possible to find help raising healthy kids in devoted sports coaches, church leaders, parents of friends, and mentors in our community.

5

RELATIONSHIPS ARE THE KEY TO BUSINESS

If someone asked me what the key to my business success was, I would tell them it's all about relationships. Relationships are how I got into business, how I grew my business, and how I continue to grow my business. Relationships are the key.

The senior executive I connected with in Waco, Texas, opened the door for me to start my career. His phone call to Darryl Nelson set me on a path that led me to where I am today. I said yes, but it wasn't a hard yes. I needed a good job and he offered one.

After moving to Burley, Idaho, I started working with my old friend, Greg Cunnington. We had a good relationship, sharing leads and supporting each other.

Right from the beginning of my insurance career, I built relationships with my clients. I got to know them, their families, their businesses, and their needs. I genuinely cared about them, and they could tell. I didn't try to sell them insurance that only benefited me and my pocketbook, but tailored my offer to fit them and their needs. I genuinely liked them, and they knew it.

I can't emphasize enough that I cared about them. I love people. I love to get to know them, find out about their lives, families, kids, beliefs, struggles, and triumphs. Everybody I meet becomes my friend.

And genuine friendship breeds loyalty.

Now don't misunderstand my motives. I did not build friendships in order to gain customers. I built friendships because I like people. And the result of those friendships was gaining and keeping customers. Even when I was the "big boss" of an insurance agency, I met and got to know all of our customers.

But that is jumping ahead.

Once we moved to Burley, I found that a good portion of the farmers and workers were self-employed and had no insurance. That worked in both of our favors. I gained a customer and they got much-needed insurance. I traveled to farms and homes in the late afternoons, evenings, and Saturdays, meeting with genuine salt-of-the-earth working men and women. I was proud to be able to help them better their lives and take away some of their financial fears.

By the time I was 27 years old, I was so successful in Burley that I opened my own office. My first hire was another guy to be a salesman with me. We did well.

After five years of establishing myself in Burley and the surrounding area, I received a call from a Blue Shield representative who covered our area. They had heard about me, a young, successful, motivated insurance broker, and wondered if I would be interested in selling group benefit products. I looked into it and decided it was a good idea. One of the perks of selling insurance to businesses was the hours. You could connect with business clients during business hours instead of in the evenings when people were off work. The other perk was the size of the accounts and subsequent commissions.

We started selling small group benefits to small businesses around the area. I liked it and not many people were doing it. Eventually, I quit selling individual life insurance and went purely to employee benefits and never looked back.

As I got deeper into group insurance benefits, I found other companies that could offer things my customers needed. I eventually sold for multiple group insurance companies, however, I only worked with those that valued agents and customers. I wanted to represent companies that had the same values and heart as I do.

> # The insurance companies I worked with needed to put customers and their needs first.

One company I stopped selling for was hard to work with. They weren't terrible or crooks or just in it for the money, but they were not flexible. They couldn't help me when I needed it, and in turn, couldn't help me help my customers.

On the other side of the coin, I had a few companies that would bend over backward to work with me. One time I had a customer with very unique needs. They wanted to be competitive and offer their employees excellent health insurance and other benefits. They reached out to me to help them find just the right insurance. After I met with the vice president and talked to him about what I could offer, he gave me the list of benefits he wanted to offer his employees. I was intrigued and challenged. I told him I would work hard to get him exactly what he wanted but couldn't guarantee it. He told me he appreciated my honesty. I got back to my office and dove into the challenge. One of the medical benefit companies I represented had helped me out before when I needed something specific. I picked up the phone and called my contact at that company. Two and a half weeks later, after many conversations, I had exactly what my customer needed. I called his direct line at work with the good news. I knew I had made a customer for life, thanks to the flexibility of that particular insurance company.

In 1987, one of the senior executives of Blue Shield of Idaho contacted me. He had just taken the position of vice president of operations in their corporate office in Lewiston, Idaho. He offered me a job as sales representative of the entire company. They wanted to open a district office in Twin Falls, Idaho. He wanted me to get it off the ground and after a couple of years have me shift to the corporate office in Lewiston.

Carla and I talked about it. We weighed the pros and cons and decided I should go for it, with the understanding that I would commute the 45 minutes to Twin Falls so she could keep the kids near their grandparents. By this time, we had bought a house in Burley and the kids had their grandparents, cousins, friends, and a loving community nearby.

I spread the word that my insurance business was up for sale and transitioned to Blue Shield. Very quickly I received a purchase offer and accepted. It wasn't a ton, but it was enough.

Success as a Blue Shield Employee

In a very short period of time, I turned the Blue Shield Twin Falls office into their largest sales division. I was an employee, earning part salary and part commission with full benefits. Because my pay was based on how successful I was, I worked hard—harder than I had as a business owner. My team and I rocked it.

About five months in—six at the most—the vice president of marketing at the headquarters in Lewiston called me and said, "I don't want to wait a year or two. Can you move here now?"

That was a shock to our well-laid plans, but I talked to Carla and told her they wanted us to move sooner. The man who wanted me up there told me that if and when he moved up to the position of president when the current president retired, he would offer me his position. Even with this potential incentive, there were some serious things we needed to think through. The pay they were offering was not commission based and it was a 30% pay cut from what I was currently making. We had two little kids at the time—AJ and Livi—with one on the way, and we'd be moving them over eight hours from their grandparents, cousins, and everything they had known. We had never lived near Lewiston and didn't have a community or even know anyone outside of work.

I have always been thankful for Carla. She has a different way of looking at things than I do and also a ton of wisdom. After thinking about it, discussing it, and counting the cost, she agreed that this was the next step. So we put our house up for sale and while she juggled caring for the two kids, being pregnant, packing, and moving, I transitioned to Lewiston to start my job and begin looking for housing.

Over the next few years, I turned the sales and marketing department for Blue Shield of Idaho into a rock star. We did better than they'd ever done. But I am quick to admit that I didn't do it alone.

This story once again comes back to relationships. It took me a few months to build a solid team. I had to let a few people go, hire and train some, and stoke the fire under the ones I kept. But by the end of that first season, I had an amazing team that I knew would work hard and be successful.

People ask me how I did it. I like to say that a blind pig finds an acorn every once in a while, so I'd always just keep rooting around. But what it really comes down to is hard work, a great team, and building relationships with customers—even corporate ones.

It was during this time in my little family's life that Carla was the real hero. I was putting in ridiculous hours, traveling all over the state, and when at home, I was on the phone (amazingly, cordless by this time) constantly. She was our at-home, work-super-hard queen raising our three kids, AJ, Livi, and Trevor, who had joined the family soon after we moved to Lewiston. She was dealing with school issues (AJ and Livi were in early elementary), difficult neighbors, meeting our kids' various needs, stimulating their adventurous curiosity, and helping them learn and develop life skills. She handled everything at home and she did it well.

After two years of my grueling but successful schedule, I decided that I needed to talk to the executive management about my pay. I had been making a salary with no meaningful incentives. I knew what my team was making and what the sales teams in offices across the state were making and it was more than me. And not by just a little bit.

I talked to them and told them I had to make more. I would like to make a commission, but at least a pay raise would be better than nothing. They wouldn't hear of it.

Then the guy who had brought me on, the vice president of operations, had a potential opportunity to become president. I was excited; all the hard work and sacrifice would be worth it.

The board had their meeting to decide who the next president would be and to my great delight the vice president was chosen. And then, two days later, I accidentally found out that he offered another guy his old job—the one he had promised to me.

That ended my interest in being at Blue Shield.

Looking back on it now, I am grateful for what happened. I wouldn't be where I am today if I had kept climbing the corporate ladder and would not have had the opportunity to build a family business, start another career, or raise my kids in the beautiful community of Meridian, Idaho. In fact, I am so grateful for what didn't happen that when discouragements come to others, I tell them my story about how sometimes blessings come in the disguise of rejection and disappointments.

> **Closed doors (even ones that get slammed in our faces) encourage us to search for other opportunities.**

And so over the next six months, I started looking for other opportunities.

There were a couple of companies in Boise, Idaho, that looked into hiring me but didn't end up following through. I am thankful for them because it made me look into Boise more. I finally found a company that was the second-largest brokerage company in the nation at that time. It was over 150 years old and had been privately held the whole time with a stellar reputation.

They had a property casualty insurance office in Boise that was a division of their Seattle office—one of their most successful offices in the country. Some of their clients were huge companies like Boeing. They wanted to start a benefits operation in Boise as well. I crossed paths with a guy named Tom Treves. We connected and became good friends. He could tell that I would be a good fit to head up their new benefits office in southern Idaho. They offered me the job.

Once again, I went to Carla and got her wisdom. This transition had very few drawbacks. She had full faith in me that I would make my office as successful as I had in Burley and Lewiston.

Boise, Idaho, here we come.

Success at Johnson and Higgins

I started with Johnson and Higgins in August of 1991. When I began, they didn't have a benefits operation in Boise, Idaho, although nationally they had a big one. Within a few years, my office had grown into the second-largest benefits brokerage in the state.

They were an easy company to work for. It was a great place with awesome people. I was in charge of my own office and that office was a division of the Seattle office, which was run by amazing people who really cared. I had a good relationship with everyone and if I ever had a problem come up, I knew they would help me solve it.

Not only that, but they wanted me to have every tool in order to be successful. I remember one particular tool: the cell phone. Though it had been invented a while back, it was just coming into mainstream use. This device was not the sleek little touch screen iPhone you are probably picturing in your head. This cell phone was a brick. It was about 10 x 2 x 4 inches, weighed almost a pound, and had an antenna that extended another 18 inches. But though it was huge, it was portable. After spending almost a decade having to stop at phone booths or public pay phones to call clients before meeting them, or Carla to tell her I'm on my way home, or corporate to give them updates, I was ready for this new technology. I made an official request to the Seattle office for a cell phone and they immediately approved it.

That small bit of technology changed my life. Though when I received the first bill, I nearly had a heart attack. Back then, when you used your cell phone through different cell towers, they charged you for every different area you traveled through. That first monthly bill was over $600, and that was in the early 1990s. But the corporate office didn't even blink. They faithfully paid my monthly bill and I gratefully used that cell phone whenever I needed it.

My job with them lasted seven years.

Around 1996, I was made vice president of operations because the guy who'd been in that role got transferred to San Diego. I was more than ready for that position and loved the fact that I could get to know everyone on every level, helping them rise to their full potential.

Johnson and Higgins was my dream job. It was the best place I had ever worked. My position was salaried, and when I got promoted to vice president of operations, it increased to six figures for the first time in my life. It was enjoyable to not have to worry about finances, be able to invest in other markets, and be generous by helping people and organizations in need.

Working for Johnson and Higgins was fulfilling. If what happened next hadn't occurred, I would have worked for them forever. I loved my role. Being a division of the Seattle office was extremely beneficial. The people I worked with were amazing. And I loved my clients. It was the perfect job. Turning the benefits office into a well-oiled operation kept me on my toes but it was the challenge and goal that made me thrive.

Little did I know that everything was about to change.

Everything Changes

Early one morning in the beginning of 1997, I got a call at home from the New York corporate office. They said, "Hey Ron. Go into the office early this morning and open your email."

A call like that was strange and it made me nervous. I replied, "Okay, I can do that, but what will I find? What's going on?"

They didn't answer my questions. "Just go in there and open your email. When the staff gets in, you can have a meeting and announce what it is about."

Getting ready as fast as I could, I headed into the office a good 45 minutes before anyone else would be there. After letting myself in, I headed back to my corner office without even bothering to turn on the lights. While I walked past the dark and quiet reception area and past all of the empty cubicles and offices, I speculated on what the email would be about. Was my life about to change?

Sitting down at my desk, I started up my computer and opened my email program. There it was, right at the top of my dozen or so unread emails, marked URGENT. I clicked the email open and glanced through it. Shock coursed through my body. I had expected something bad, but this was beyond believable. Starting from the beginning again, I read the email word for word.

They had sold the company.

Nothing would be the same again. Johnson and Higgins had been around for 150 years. They were the second largest in the nation and the email announced that they had sold the company to the largest insurance brokerage company in the nation for a whopping $1.2 billion.

What were they thinking? The company buying Johnson and Higgins was our archenemy. We would say, "They're the terrible guys. We're the good guys." It felt like a betrayal. I couldn't believe it because literally 10 days before that email announcement, I had been in Arizona at a conference where all the executives were all "rah-rah-rah" and "go-go-go" like nothing was wrong. Obviously, they couldn't say anything, but just that short time later, I got the email with the announcement.

I sat in shock for who knows how long. But the sounds of my team arriving and getting ready to settle into their desks to get working shook me from my daze. I needed to talk to them.

Calling a meeting as soon as everyone had arrived, I broke the news. There was not much I could tell them. The company had been sold.

My team needed reassurance that they would be okay, but I couldn't give it to them. I didn't even know if they could keep their jobs, let alone what the future would hold. These were people I cared about who provided for their families. What would happen to them?

Straight after the meeting, I called one of the owners in Seattle. "What's going on? You're selling to the enemy! What is this?" He was one of the voting members at the time. I found out later that he walked away with $50 million.

For six years I thought I was going to be at this company forever and now they wanted me to sign on and partner with the opposing team. I couldn't picture myself switching to the other side.

Later, I found out that selling Johnson and Higgins was not an integrity issue. There were no underhanded deals. It was simply that all the executive-level people were offered the chance to walk away filthy rich. Unfortunately, the rest of us were left working for the enemy.

When the details finally came in, Johnson and Higgins offered me $30,000 to sign a noncompete agreement for the new company.

Carla and I were really shaken up. As always, there were positives and negatives to both the decisions facing us: Do we sign the noncompete, start working for the enemy company, and see where it goes? Or do we walk away completely and start from the ground up with my own new company?

Looking back now, I guess there was a third option, but after the abrupt ending at Johnson and Higgins, I didn't want to join another established company and have the same thing happen to me again.

One of the executive guys called me in early July, just a few weeks before the company sale closing. He said, "Hey Ron, you haven't signed the noncompete yet. Why not?" I told him I was really struggling with it. He said, "Ron, grab Carla, get on a plane, and come over here. Let's sit down and talk."

I said, "Okay, we will be there tonight."

That evening I sat across from him in his office in Seattle, while Carla waited anxiously at the hotel. He suggested, "Ron, just take their money and run. You and Carla take your family on a great vacation somewhere." But at that point I was making six figures a year so $30,000 was not a huge incentive. But besides the money, I had a hard time picturing myself working for the new company.

I had told the guy we talked to that I would talk to Carla and think about it overnight. He was a good friend, but this was my future—not his.

Carla and I spent hours talking about it. Though we did weigh the pros and cons, what it came down to was that we did not feel comfortable working for the new company. We decided that saying *no*, even though it was hard and I would let some people down, was more important than giving in to the pressure. I felt like my integrity was at stake. Making that decision brought the peace that I had been lacking for the last few months. The next morning I met with my Seattle executive friend again. I told him, "I'm not signing it. I'm done."

He was not surprised. He told me he understood but asked me to hand him the keys to my corporate car and informed me that I was not allowed to go into my office back home to even get my personal stuff. They would have it boxed up and sent to me. I had worked in corporate enough to know how it works, but it was still a shock to me because I was the vice president of sales. It was my office. But nothing drives home the truth better than being treated like a criminal. The business did not belong to me.

Before the trip to Seattle and the subsequent decision, I had been evaluating our next step. I had started talking with Bob, an independent insurance agent in town. One of his best salesmen had recently left to work for another broker so he was looking for a change and maybe a partner.

As we connected, the idea of partnering with him and starting a new insurance brokerage company came up. I had successfully done it before and knew that I had a jump start on finding clients. I figured that if I declined working for the new company that bought Johnson and Higgins, at least a few of the clients I had previously with Johnson and Higgins would join me in my new company. We got together and talked and agreed on every aspect. I could work with this guy and he liked me too. It looked like we would make a good fit to start an agency.

Bob and I spent the next month or two talking about the possibility of starting an insurance agency as equal partners.

> **Loyalty and rewarding hard work were the two most important components to me as I built this business that could potentially be my legacy.**

One of the important pieces I wanted to implement in my own company came from my experience with both Blue Shield and Johnson and Higgins. In both of those companies, I had started out with very little, poured my heart and soul into growing what I had been given and grown it into an extremely successful division. And in the end, it had not mattered. I lost it all because of the decisions of the executives. I wanted to do it differently. I wanted to establish loyalty in both the way the business was run and with our employees right from the start.

Thankfully, Bob heard me. Those things were important to him as well and we talked for long hours about how to establish those values.

The day Carla and I flew back from Seattle after officially declining the offer, I called Bob and said, "Let's do it."

We dove in headfirst, getting our new business off the ground. We made sure to tackle the practical aspects of starting a business the right way. We worked hard to find just the right name that would explain who and what we were and would work if we ever wanted to sell the business down the road. We also found a lawyer who was practiced in drawing up partnership agreements.

Bob already had a good-sized office near the famous BSU football stadium with the blue turf, with an area I could move a desk into and work from. His current assistant was also able to work for me and knew how to keep the books and manage the accounts. We were set. I was so excited to own my own business again.

We officially started Western Benefit Solutions (WBS) in July 1997. Year we married :)

Tom Treves, my friend who had introduced me to Johnson and Higgins, had moved temporarily to Boise to run the office after I left. He called me out of the blue toward the end of summer. He said, "Hey Ron, can you come by the office? I just want to talk to you."

To avoid making it awkward for those former team members who had chosen to stay, I showed up late when everybody else had gone home. We sat down to catch up and I asked him how the transition was going. He professed, "Most clients said they wanted to do business with you, so I didn't get very far with them. In fact, I don't have enough work here so I'm returning to Seattle." He wasn't upset with me. He knew that insurance is a relationship business. My clients were loyal. They had told him, "No, we do business with Ron. Who are you?"

That was encouraging to me and after contacting my former clients, 80-90 percent of them came over to my business within a few months. I was so grateful that I never signed that noncompete.

Over the next year, WBS exploded.

The Lesser-Known Key to Business Success

As I look back over my career, it strikes me that there are three major keys to success. Two I have talked about extensively. Building relationships is at the heart of a good business. Working hard and establishing a good work ethic from your employees is the second major factor. But there is a very important third key: timing.

> **Timing is something people don't think about much.**

When planning anything big, you need to ask, "Is now the right time?" You need to look into the market, the culture, world events, and supply and demand. You need to think about things like globalization, communication, marketing, the economy, and technology. Those things can be huge, complicated, and potentially scary, but they can't be overlooked or brushed aside.

For example, opening a Blockbuster video store in 2004 would have spelled disaster. In 2004, Blockbuster was at its peak but on the edge of a cliff. Both Netflix and Redbox had come out and the price, the location, the ease, and the lack of late fees took a major portion of the video store's business. After the Netflix and Redbox craze died down, streaming services began to grow, followed by digital movie downloads. In fact, almost 20 years later, there is only one Blockbuster still in operation. But at its peak in 2004, there were over 9,000 Blockbuster stores generating around $5.9 billion annually.

My youngest was born in 1992 and that was the year the internet started. By 1997, about the time we started Western Benefit Solutions (WBS), it was really starting to be functional. The timing was incredible in the insurance business. All of a sudden, we could get access to data and information that insurance brokerage firms previously had to pay national companies a lot of money to obtain. Most small insurance companies wouldn't get the information because it was just too expensive.

In 1997, as we started and established WBS, we took advantage of everything the internet had to offer, including researching the companies we wanted to reach out to and using that information to put together initial proposals that fit them like a glove. Between that and establishing relationships with the decision-makers, we were able to catch really big fish. We offered them exactly what they needed and we both benefited.

WBS continued to grow by leaps and bounds. It was the right time in the market, as Idaho had taken off and was experiencing a business boom. I established a niche in the public sector. I was able to offer benefit solutions to various counties, school districts, and large corporations.

In 1992, when I was still working for Johnson and Higgins, I had become the broker for the Statewide School Association. It was one of the largest plans in the state and they had never had a broker before. I brought that account with me to WBS. We also got the Albertsons account and other equally large companies.

Even though we were well on our way to becoming the largest benefit insurance brokers in the state and one of the biggest in the northwest, we made sure to never lose sight of the foundational values that WBS had been established on: loyalty and relationships.

Building Your Business on Loyalty

The first person who worked for us was an employee named Peggy Kearsley. I love Peggy and her family to this day. When she started working for us, she and her husband had only been married a couple years. She was a young gal who worked extremely hard and initially worked as an account manager, assistant, and bookkeeper for WBS.

One day, she and her husband asked to talk to me. They came in to announce that they were expecting a child and she'd have to quit. She started crying because she loved working for us and knew that she couldn't raise a family and work at WBS full time. I said, "You don't need to quit." I told her she could keep working on the books from home.

At the time, working from home was quite unusual. This was almost three decades before the COVID pandemic, which made working from home normal and common. Women who were raising kids didn't keep their regular jobs and do them from home. It just didn't happen.

But it was important to me to be loyal and to reward Peggy's loyalty. I knew we could find someone else to do Peggy's job, but I wanted Peggy to do Peggy's job and I knew she could do it from home.

She went on to have four kids and she continued working with me for a total of 18 years.

As I have mentioned (more than a few times), relationships are the key to business. Not just the insurance business, but most businesses. Businesses are run by people and people are relational at their core. Over the years of working with customers, salesmen, friends, and family, and in my community, I have found that investing in relationships brings not only fulfillment and joy, but also good business.

One of the things I did that was different from other insurance brokers was to establish relationships with most of the clients who came through our office. Even if their main salesman was someone else, I would contact them, make sure they were being taken care of, and get to know them.

In fact once, one of our bigger accounts called me up to tell me the salesman from WBS wasn't getting stuff done. I responded, "I appreciate it and I'll get the right people in there." I made sure to take care of them.

My salesmen were taken care of as well, not just in pay but also with training. We wanted them to have the same values that established WBS and made it a powerhouse. We had regular meetings, challenged them to raise the standard, and provided tools to help them be successful. We also had a good support staff team.

> # To encourage employees financially, we gave them trips, incentives, and goals.

Here was my model: we paid the brokers extremely well so we would have good brokers. I handled my block of business with key clients, which covered the cost of expenses and over-head. Then, the money we made from the clients of the sales-people covered the salespeople's commissions.

We paid our support staff well—the assistants, underwriters, accountants, account managers, and office managers. And be-cause of that, we got some of the best employees. In fact, during the Great Recession between December 2007 and June 2009, not only did we pay well, but we gave them raises and bonuses. They did not worry about losing their jobs like so many other employ-ees in the community.

In 2009, I became the sole owner of WBS when I bought out Bob for the predetermined amount that we had agreed upon in writing during the early creation of our partnership. Having an agreed-upon percentage of the annual income when we first started the business kept things neat and organized legally when it was time to make a change. Though the process was fraught with relational challenges and awkwardness, it worked out in the end.

Between 1997 and 2012, Western Benefit Solutions took off like a rocket. At our peak we employed a total of 18 support staff and salesmen. As we continued to grow, we realized that WBS had a unique niche in the Idaho insurance market. There were small brokers and large brokerage firms, but we played a different role. We found that we could provide our customers with resources and benefits like big national brokerages, but were personable and relational like the mom-and-pop agencies.

Right from the start of WBS, we saw steady upward growth that averaged around 16% per year. This was caused not just by the growing market in Idaho but also because of my past experience. I had seen the benefits and struggles that Johnson and Higgins had encountered being one of the big national insurance brokerages. As a not-too-big but not-too-small brokerage, WBS was able to take advantage of the strengths of both the big and small and address those struggles. Western Benefit Solutions was in the perfect position for continued growth and success.

6

DO WHAT IS BEST FOR THE CUSTOMER

Throughout the prosperous years in insurance, we made sure to do what was best for the customer. In return, customers have stayed with us year after year. There are three important factors to focus on in business that result in doing what's best for the customer.

Integrity

Integrity is critical to running a successful business and keeping customers. We made sure that we were always forthright, honest, and above board.

Countless times over the years, I have been told that our customers appreciate how we communicated with them, were honest with them, and weren't "shady." We also made it a point to not "smear" the competition. We would matter-of-factly share the differences between what we offered and what they offered, but because we chose to put the customer first, we could offer better services, options, and prices.

Personal integrity was critically important to me too. I knew that God would not bless me if I was dishonest. Because of my personal connections with 95 percent of our clients, that carried over into my business dealings. I could not be underhanded at work and be honest at home. My work life was my personal life.

Loyalty

Being loyal to our customers is the second practice we have followed in our business dealings. The *New Oxford American Dictionary* defines loyalty as *giving or showing firm and constant support or allegiance to a person or institution.*

Loyalty goes both ways. We made sure to constantly support and align ourselves with our customers. If our client had a problem, we had a problem. This was also fostered by building relationships. As a businessperson, I always wanted to have a vested interest in the success of my client's companies as well as the success of the individuals within the company. If we could make them more successful or save them money, I worked extremely hard to accomplish that. Or you might say, I worked my tail off.

One of the first things I did to connect with clients was to take them to a fancy dinner. Going out to dinner had many benefits. Over dinner I could establish generosity, encouraging them to get the best entrée, drink, and dessert. I could build relationships, asking them about their family, story, and passions. And I could hear their insurance needs and let them know that I could work with them and help them resolve any issues.

I also made a point to support the company or an organization close to their heart with donations. One school district we had as a client was moving into a new building and needed a sign in their boardroom. I heard about the need and decided we would donate one. We spent $5,000 to order a large metal sign exactly as they wanted it. The sign was a beautiful masterpiece. And in return, they put a small plaque under the sign that said that WBS had donated it.

Over the years, I have built lasting friendships. Even when I could no longer offer them business solutions, most of my clients have remained good friends.

Problem-Solving

My years spent working for Blue Shield of Idaho provided the education that I consider my "college degree." Those years of working closely with executives, underwriters, and actuaries taught me how and what the insurance companies could do for their clients.

Because of that experience, I knew how much wiggle room I had (a lot) with large insurance carriers on behalf of my clients. I made sure to establish relationships with the right people at these companies who could work with me and personalize insurance options for my clients. I would reach out to them to find for my clients exactly what they needed in particular situations. Because of this, we all benefited; the insurance company got customers, I made my clients happy, and my clients' needs were covered.

One of the big fish that I landed with this principle was Albertsons Corporation, the huge grocery chain headquartered in Boise. When Bob and I had partnered initially and started WBS, he provided a small portion of the insurance needs for

Albertsons. After Bob and I parted ways and I bought him out, I decided to reach out to Albertsons to see if we could offer benefits to cover all or most of their insurance needs.

I set up a meeting with the Albertsons CFO. They had just had a major change in management and this was the first time I had met him. We had a good meeting and I explained what I could do for him and how I could save him a ton of money by consolidating the insurance benefits they offered.

He was impressed and surprised not just by my knowledge, but also by how much I could possibly save the company. They gave me the go-ahead to see what I could get for them from the insurance carriers. I went to one particular carrier that I had a really good relationship with and asked them what they could do for me and Albertsons. This carrier very much wanted the business and bent over backward to give us exactly what Albertsons needed for a great price.

The insurance carrier even paid for an HR support person to work for Albertsons so the benefits and employees' needs would be more than covered. I have never had that happen before or since, with an insurance carrier being that invested in keeping a client.

That was the beginning of a beautiful relationship, not only with the Albertsons company but also the individuals running the company. We eventually brokered all their insurance needs. We saved them so much money that the running joke every year at the annual trustees' meeting was how WBS was going to save them another million in the coming year. We also got so involved that we were one of the sponsors for their charity events.

Another way we helped solve our clients' problems was by offering free educational seminars. While in the midst of growing

WBS, we held conferences every six months to educate people on various insurance-related issues. In the beginning, we had a good turnout and people really appreciated hearing from insurance experts. However, once the Affordable Care Act (Obamacare) was established and the rules got much more complicated, we found that double the people were requesting to attend. People were desperate to understand the complexities of the new health insurance laws.

This was another opportunity for mutual benefit; we became established as leaders in the industry which led to more clients, and our customers learned how to work with the laws in the insurance field. Education always helps clients feel empowered.

The other thing we offered our clients to help them solve their problems was a great team at WBS who helped them do their jobs more effectively. We tried to hire people who knew their stuff and had the drive and desire to learn every nuance. We had an amazing team who not only partnered with us, their bosses, but also partnered with our clients to help them and treat them the way we did.

Doing the Right Thing in Business

Doing the right thing in business sounds simple but sometimes is not clear. One of the ways we made sure to do the right thing was to prioritize who and what came first in our business. Without customers, we had no business, so they were the natural priority. Everything else came after the customers and what they needed to succeed. We felt that by partnering with them, they could experience the loyalty and integrity that was so important to us.

We kept getting new clients because of word of mouth. Our customers knew we would take care of them, and they could confidently refer us to others. One of the best ways we got referrals was when an HR employee of one of our clients started working for another company and wanted to keep us as their insurance broker. They wanted us to take over the accounts for the new company because they trusted us to do the right thing.

Another way we did the right thing was by focusing on people, not the finances. As a company, we worked hard at WBS to make our business about people. We focused on keeping the customers happy and being generous with them. This also meant we needed to do the same with our employees and our sales team. Generosity breeds wealth, and not just financial wealth. I am talking about relational wealth, time wealth, and mental health wealth.

When you live a life of generosity, you are wealthy.

Lastly, doing the right thing included being generous with nonprofit organizations and encouraging our employees to be generous as well. During the WBS boom, we gave our time, heart, and resources to organizations that reflected our values. I truly took my business relationships personally due to my background and growing up the way I did. It was a good thing that Carla was such a wonderful parent because it helped me keep a stable family in perspective too.

As a child, I remember one incident that impacted me. My mom went to the dentist because she had a toothache. The dentist checked it out and saw that it was a pretty big cavity. He warned her how much it would cost to fill it even while insisting that she needed to or she could lose the tooth. Cavities and fillings were not new to my mom. She had grown up only seeing the dentist when things got bad and toothaches became too much to handle. She wanted something different for me and my siblings.

She decided after she got her filling that we all needed to see the dentist for a cleaning and a checkup. No one in the family was having a dental emergency, but my mom wanted to do what she could to avoid one in the future. She talked to the dentist about seeing all of us. His response was surprising. He almost wouldn't see us because he told her it would cost too much. She insisted on making appointments for each of us.

After getting home, she called her brother in Washington to ask for a loan. She didn't know how much it would cost, but she didn't have anything extra. Her brother agreed to loan her the money. After our four appointments, during which they found a few cavities and filled them, they gave the bill to my mom. It was over $1,000. She got the money from her brother and paid the dental bill.

Over the next year and a half, she saved up what she could from each paycheck to pay her brother back. Once she had painstakingly saved up every penny she owed, she wrote the check for the full amount, put it in an envelope with a thank-you note, and popped it in the mail to her brother. Six days later, she received a phone call from him. He told her that he had ripped up the check.

My mom cried.

My uncle's generosity left a mark on me. I knew even as a small child that I wanted to help other people the way my mom had been helped. Carla and I had that chance when I heard about

Regence Blue Shield's fund called Caring Foundation. Regence Caring Foundation for Children, Inc., ran for 22 years and helped over 31,000 low-income kids get regular dental checkups, cleanings, and fillings. They covered up to $1,000 per child per year.

The vision and practical help Regence offered immediately hooked me. It brought me back to that time when we got help going to the dentist. We started giving regularly and a couple of years later, I was asked to join the board. Once a year we had a meeting when we got to hear directly from impacted families. They would share their stories and how grateful they were to get financial help for their children's dental needs. I wasn't the only one who left those meetings having shed a few tears.

The WBS team volunteering to answer calls
at Idaho Public Television's telethon.

We helped other nonprofits as well. We didn't always give regularly, but our favorite thing to do was help with fundraising events like charity auctions. Every Christmas our office also donated toys to kids in need. We liked to participate in practical ways and got our employees involved as well.

> ## We knew that being generous blesses both the recipients and the giver.

By 2004, Western Benefit Solutions was fulfilling every one of my business dreams. I was making enough money to be generous with my salesmen, employees, family, and the nonprofits near and dear to my heart. And I was working hard at a business I loved that helped people.

We were doing so well I had even started investing our extra income in real estate. When I started thinking about the future and retirement, I knew that I wanted to invest in a market that was not client driven. I had experienced the shock of losing big clients for one reason or another and knew that finding an investment that was not based on how the client felt was important. Now don't get me wrong—more often than not, I was the recipient of clients leaving other insurance brokers and joining WBS, but it was important to me to diversify.

What that desire for diversification started was the beginning of something huge and life changing for me and for my family.

7

BE CONTENT AND DON'T ALWAYS SAY NO, BUT MOSTLY SAY NO

When I started thinking about investing in real estate personally, I thought about what most people first consider: buying homes or apartments and renting them out. I really didn't know anything else.

Fortunately, I came across a couple of articles about self-storage and looked into it. What I found was surprising. The return on investment was phenomenal. They required little staffing, were in huge demand, and had low turnover. I decided that self-storage was perfect for me.

As luck would have it, one day in the office, my partner Bob and I were having lunch. He knew I was looking into real estate and I told him what I was thinking about. "I did a ton of research and I think it is a perfect thing to invest in. Now all I need is to find a facility for sale."

Bob, who had been eating quietly, looked up, startled. He set his sandwich down and immediately told me, "I have a friend who owns a storage facility in Idaho Falls. He is in financial trouble and needs to sell it. Maybe you guys could help each other out."

> ## That storage business, with about 125 units, became my first diversified investment.

Because of the staff I had with WBS, I was able to bring the books and management of the facility to my office. It was a fairly smooth transition. It worked out so well that my son AJ was also interested in investing, so he and I started looking for other facilities. The next one was in Walla Walla, Washington, then in Pendleton, Oregon, and then in Sandpoint, Idaho.

By 2007, we owned four storage facilities that ranged from 100 units to 300 units.

Because I had an insurance business that was doing well, we didn't take any money from the storage facilities. Everything they generated we put back into them: paying down the loans, improving the buildings and grounds, and optimizing expenses.

With those facilities, I decided to become a learner. I pored over everything I could find about self-storage as a business. I even took time to attend the self-storage conference held in Las Vegas every year. I constantly analyzed what I could do better, how I could improve the return on investment, and what the short-term and long-term investment would look like.

AJ and I started with only a few storage facilities and learned everything from the ground up.

We had only those four storage businesses until 2012. And even though I know that owning four facilities sounds like a lot, I found it really wasn't. Looking back, I see that starting small, learning how to handle the issues that came up and how to improve the return on investment, helped me get a foundation for the future when self-storage would become my major business.

Western Benefit Solutions Officially Becomes a Family Business

AJ graduated from BYU in 2005. He wanted to join me at WBS right away, but I thought it would be a good idea for him to get some experience first with another company. He started with

Aflac and worked with them for about a year and then phased in to WBS.

AJ did a good job as a salesman. He worked hard to find clients and in the beginning I went out with him on lead calls to help him learn how to do it and close the deals. He was very teachable and loved learning. Pretty soon he took off and I let him fly.

Having AJ on the team was amazing. He has a serious work ethic, has vision to grow and expand the company, and is easy to work with. I say all of that in the present, because even now, over a decade later, he is still amazing to work with and I benefit from his drive and focus.

As he was growing up, we had to find the right school path for him. What he struggled with in school has become a huge asset. People with dyslexia have a hard time in a traditional school system that is created for visual learners who can sit for long periods of time. Anyone who does not fit that mold struggles.

But AJ's dyslexia gives him an advantage in the world of business. He has the ability to see vision and purpose, knows how to get there, and finds the right people with the right skills to support that vision. He is humble and relational, knowing that everybody struggles in some way. He turned out to be not only a great salesman but an excellent manager and leader.

Livi brought another important person into our business. She didn't hire him—she started dating him and ended up marrying him. Sam Whitaker and Livi started dating after she came home from New York. He was getting his degree in finance from Boise State University and was very business minded. We needed him.

Sam came in to help WBS. He helped with accounting and bookkeeping as well as internal processes. He has a good head for that sort of thing—finance and details. He could help us with the nitty-gritty of our projects, something that does not come naturally to the Osbornes. He compliments us well.

Having a son and a son-in-law working in the business was fun. I really enjoyed going to work and knowing that two family members I loved and admired would be there. Helping them provide for their families was an added bonus.

The years from 1998 to 2011 rolled along with blessings and success. By the end of 2011, WBS was one of the major players in providing benefit solutions to many companies, not only in Idaho but all around the United States.

In March of 2012, a gentleman from the international insurance brokerage firm Arthur J. Gallagher & Co. reached out to me. They wanted to know if I would be interested in selling Western Benefits Solutions. I told them clearly, "Nope. I'm not interested in selling it." They understood but still expressed the desire to talk to me. They had flown up from Texas, and I didn't mind meeting with them for lunch to just hear them out, especially if they picked up the tab.

AJ and I met with them and I really enjoyed talking to these guys. They explained Gallagher, its vision, its purpose, and its focus on clients. They talked about how Gallagher was run and how it helped people. I think they knew what was important to me as a legacy, if I were to sell WBS, my baby. At the end of it all I told them, "You guys wouldn't be willing to pay what I want in order to consider selling."

They asked what I was thinking.

I quickly started running numbers in my head, kept upping the number, and then added a couple million to that just to hit it out of the ballpark. I told them, "It would probably be in this range . . ."

To our shock, they responded, "Okay, I think we can work with that."

As AJ and I drove back to the office in stunned silence, I thought, "Shoot! I made up the highest number I could. I'm obviously too low."

To continue the process, we hired a guy out of Minnesota who brokered these kinds of deals. I wanted to make sure all our bases were covered by someone who could represent us well.

I told this broker, "Go see what you can work out with these guys, but here's the minimum price . . ." And I upped it a few million more. I said, "If they can't do that, I don't want to do it."

Don't get me wrong, I wasn't greedy. But I was really happy with WBS and was only willing to sell it if they could pay top dollar. By paying a high price, it showed that they would cherish and grow it. That was the only way I could know that Gallagher really wanted my business, my employees, and my clients. And they were who I cared about.

My broker succeeded.

Arthur J. Gallagher & Company officially bought Western Benefit Solutions on December 1, 2012.

Gallagher wanted AJ and me to stay on for an initial three years. They knew that transitioning slowly and my staying in touch with our clients was super important for future success. I ended up staying for a total of seven years, moving to a PR position after the initial three years, where I didn't have to work full time.

Selling WBS to a reputable firm like Gallagher opened the possibility of jumping headfirst into another business, a business not dependent on customer whims and feelings. We could start a business dedicated 100% to self-storage.

Between March, when I first talked to Gallagher, and when we closed in December, AJ, Sam, and I spent long days, especially in the summer, at my pool planning, arranging, and structuring the new company and growth. We decided to call it Bitterroot Holdings, named after the mountains where AJ loved to hike and camp. He was fascinated by the ecosystem that the Bitterroot Mountains in Idaho create and how they have influenced the weather, topography, and culture of that area for thousands of years.

It was an amazing experience starting a business from the ground up with AJ and Sam. We each had our own unique gifts and complimented each other well.

At that point, I had the four storage companies I'd bought as personal investments that I was able to bring to Bitterroot Holdings. While it had originally been a diversification strategy, I had fallen in love with the industry and was excited for what was to come.

AJ, Sam (with his firstborn), and me at one of our
newer storage facilities a few years later.

My life and business were on an upward trajectory. I could only see good things as the business grew and our family expanded with new daughters-in-law and grandkids. However, little did I know that one of the most painful and heart-wrenching times were ahead.

8

HOLD ON IN THE TOUGH TIMES

Not many events during my lifetime have rocked my world. My father's stroke and then passing two years later was the first. I dealt with shock, grief, resentment, fear, worry, and then grief and fear again. My great-Uncle Ari's passing was the second time my world was rocked. For those two events, I didn't have a foundation to hold onto. I didn't have a family network, perspective, or faith.

My world was rocked again in October 2016. For all of those years in between, I had ups and downs, but definitely more ups than downs. Carla and I had challenges to overcome or situations to work through. Everything we went through in those in-between years we could do something about. We could make decisions, we could hire experts, we could practice, plan, or try. We had some level of control over our situations.

But the world-rocking event in fall of 2016 was completely out of my control, like when I lost my dad and uncle. All I could do was hang in there, holding on to Carla and my family.

We received a call in the wee hours of the morning. I answered the phone, bleary-eyed and worried. No one ever called us at this hour. Carla sat up next to me and waited anxiously to find out what was going on.

It was Tessa, AJ's wife. She told us that AJ had taken a bath the night before because of pain in his legs and while in the bath had become paralyzed. She called 911 and AJ had been transported to the hospital.

I knew AJ had been having some pain with his feet and legs for the last week. He had even been to the hospital because of it, but they had only given him some over-the-counter pain medication and sent him home. The doctor was clueless about what was causing the pain.

Carla and I got dressed quickly and hopped in the car. As we navigated the dark empty streets on the way to the hospital, we were both silently praying. God knew what was going on and he could lead the doctors to the answer.

Specialist after specialist examined AJ, ordering test after test. Everything came back completely normal except that he was paralyzed and in excruciating pain. The days passed and AJ kept getting worse, until he was struggling to even breathe. The doctors made the hard decision to put him under and intubate him. They needed the machines to do the job that his body couldn't do—breathe.

Family in Crisis

Each worsening step AJ went through took its toll on the entire family. Carla and I were doing what needed to be done but barely holding on. We made sure to be there for our kids, their spouses, and our grandkids.

Finally, one doctor saw AJ who had an idea what his ailment might be. He ordered tests that confirmed his diagnosis.

Tessa was home with the kids and Carla and I were with AJ at the hospital when the doctor gave us the news. We had been taking turns being at the hospital with AJ and helping with AJ and Tessa's four kids, one of whom was only 6 months old. I was also working to keep Bitterroot Holdings running smoothly.

He told us that AJ had something called Guillain-Barre' syndrome (GBS). He explained that it is an autoimmune condition where the body attacks the nerves. It usually starts in the feet and moves up the body. It can be triggered by a variety of things, including respiratory infections and vaccinations. AJ had just received a few vaccinations in preparation to go fishing in Brazil with some buddies. The doctor warned us not to look Guillain-Barre' syndrome up on the internet. He knew the information we might find would freak us out.

We resisted while he was in the room but as soon as he left, AJ grabbed his phone and typed it into Google. The doctor was right.

That day was the beginning of the worst four months I had ever experienced.

There was no good side or positive outlook for Guillain-Barré syndrome. We knew that AJ was experiencing the worst possible type of GBS, which would soon require intubation and ventilation. His body was attacking the nerve sheath around his peripheral nerves, causing weakness, severe pain, and eventually enough damage to severely limit the function of his lungs and spinal cord.

Guillain-Barré affected AJ's entire body, including his lungs, heart, and spinal cord, which cut off his ability to control his body, including speech, movement, and senses. The doctors kept him sedated, not just because he was ventilated, but because of the pain he was experiencing. On top of it all, he started having fearful hallucinations, which we later found out were caused by his pain medication.

Family Support

Our family rallied around him. We had been a tight-knit family before this, but with everything going on, I am proud to say that our kids really stepped up—Taylor especially.

Taylor and AJ had always been close, probably as a result of being the oldest and the youngest in the family. They had a special bond when they were growing up. AJ was 9 years old when Taylor was born, and right from the beginning, they were inseparable. By the time Taylor was old enough to join his siblings in their games, AJ was ready to be his pal, stick by his side, and help him when he struggled. AJ loved teaching Taylor big-kid things and anytime we needed the kids to pair up, it was always AJ's big teen hand grabbing Taylor's little kid hand.

Taylor was in his last semester at BYU in Hawaii when AJ got sick. He immediately wanted to come home, so he talked to all his professors, and they figured out a way for him to finish his classes from a distance. As soon as he had arranged that, he bought himself a ticket home. He surprised us by showing up at the hospital.

He ended up spending more hours in AJ's hospital room than anyone else, even while finishing up his classes online. He had a connection with AJ, even as AJ lay there unable to move or even breathe on his own. Taylor had an uncanny ability to know what AJ needed and was able to get through to him and calm him down when he was hallucinating. He knew what AJ was trying to communicate and had an overall calming effect on everyone in the room. Taylor was a lifesaver.

AJ ended up spending over four months in the hospital. When the raging disease finally started calming and they took him off sedation, he was still in tremendous pain, physically as well as emotionally. The future was completely unknown. AJ and Tessa asked the doctors if he would be able to walk again and they didn't have an answer.

After the hospital, he was moved to a physical rehabilitation facility where he had to relearn all of the basics: eating, walking, and talking. It was a fight that AJ woke up to every day—forcing his body to do things it could not do and pushing through the constant nerve pain that radiated through his body. I saw the most incredible strength in him during that trial but as a father, I would have done anything to have been able to take it away.

Instead, I helped where I could and made sure our business kept supporting him and his family so he could concentrate on healing. I also kept praying for him. I knew that God was with us and especially AJ.

Road to Recovery

When AJ was finally released to move back home, he still needed help with everything. Taylor moved in with AJ, Tessa, and their four kids to help Tessa with AJ's everyday challenges.

The road to recovery was long and painful for my firstborn. After a solid year, AJ was finally able to return to work part time, loaded with medication and with his legs in braces. Even now, years after his hospital stay, he is still dealing with residual physical effects from the disease, though he is a force to be reckoned with at work.

Throughout this process, I have marveled at the strength and fortitude that AJ has displayed. Even when he was on death's doorstep, he clung to hope and his family. During his long, slow recovery he pushed and pushed himself, refusing to back down or give in to the pain and frustration. He even found humor in his situation and brought us laughter and joy.

The first Christmas after his sickness, he was able to join us for dinner as a family. His nephew was zooming around the kitchen in his walker and AJ decided to "race" the almost 1-year-old. They both raced, AJ in his wheelchair and Magnus in his baby walker. Magnus won.

The road to recovery has been long and hard. AJ has learned to push through impossible odds and overcome physical and emotional hardships, learning to rely on people and family when he needs to.

Taylor, Tessa, the kids, and me with AJ still using his wheelchair.

It took about two years for him to become completely mobile again, though he will probably never walk without a limp. As I see him walking around the office as he helps grow our business, I am constantly amazed at how far he has come. His disease could have been the end of him like it was for my father. He could have left Tessa raising four kids on her own like my mom.

> # I can't imagine what would have happened if we were still in the poverty cycle.

AJ wouldn't have received the medical care that saved him, and our family might have lost everything trying to cover his medical bills and living expenses. Never have I been more thankful to have broken that mentality for my future generations.

That painful time has faded over the last couple of years, yet I am left with gratitude for what we have: a healthy three-generation family, a thriving business that can sustain us even if we can't work, and a faith to know that God has and will always take care of us.

9

KEEP A BALANCED PERSPECTIVE ABOUT GROWTH AND BLESSINGS

We established Bitterroot Holdings in 2012 and spent the next seven years (while AJ and I worked for Gallagher) to get it really rocking. AJ, Sam, and I were so excited because we all felt it was a good time to get into the storage business.

What we didn't know then was that it wasn't a *good* time to get into the storage business—it was a *brilliant* time.

Let me give you an example.

The first storage facility we built from the ground up under Bitterroot Holdings was in Meridian, Idaho. We really went all out. We tore down a house on the property and built everything else from scratch.

About five years later, I got an offer for four times what we put into it. It had quadrupled in value in those five years. I responded to the potential buyers, "I don't know who is more stupid, you or me . . . probably me for not taking the offer."

In another extremely successful venture, we partnered with other investors for the first time in Reno, Nevada, to buy a Super Kmart that had gone bankrupt. We spent $8 million and revamped it, turning it into a huge indoor storage facility. After two years, we were able to take the money out of it that we had invested.

Two years after that, we received an offer to buy it that was 8x the original price. We didn't sell.

In starting Bitterroot Holdings, we were smart and cautious but not fearful, and we trusted our timing.

> ## There could not have been a better time to get into the self-storage industry.

Growing Pains

Not every step we took or investment we made turned to gold. As we grew the business, we started looking at and thinking about other investment options. We looked into franchises, acquiring other insurance brokerages, and investing in other types of commercial real estate.

One of the ventures that did not return positive results was Anytime Fitness. We initially purchased the leases for 12 sites. After analyzing the best possible areas, we decided to open one on the west coast of Florida and one in northern Idaho. We spent months and a ton of money on renovating and equipping the two gyms. We fought to keep them open and running for almost two years but had to finally admit that they were not and would probably never be lucrative.

After months of trial, error, deliberation, and analysis, we finally made the decision to sell both Anytime Fitness locations. They were not turning a large enough profit and our focus and time needed to be spent on our other growing businesses.

We also went through a lawsuit in Florida where we lost a couple of million dollars simply by believing in someone's good word and integrity about an insurance brokerage we bought.

We found an insurance brokerage that was for sale. Their books laid out a picture showing that the potential income from the brokerage's accounts would offset the cost of the purchase. We were excited to expand our reach to a different market and continued the process to buy the company. We did our due diligence but didn't know that we were being given falsified documents.

Both Carla and I knew right after we signed the documents that we had trusted someone we should not have trusted. We both had not felt right about the decision before signing and had talked about it together. Unfortunately, it was too late and we had gone through with the purchase. Flying back and forth to Florida for hearings made me realize that this type of diversity was likely not what we wanted.

We learned many things from that experience: sometimes you pay dearly for an "education"; we shouldn't go through with a deal that feels wrong; and diversification for diversification's sake is not always a good thing.

Grow as a Learner

It is important to tackle life as a learner. The successful ventures and the unsuccessful ventures of my business career have all taught me business lessons, interpersonal lessons, and relational lessons.

When things didn't turn out like I expected them to, I have been able to keep perspective. Not becoming vice president of sales for Blue Shield of Idaho felt like the end of my career, at the time. It was not. In fact, it was the beginning of starting a highly successful insurance brokerage.

When we went through the hard time and lawsuit with the brokerage in Florida, I was able to keep perspective. I had a thriving business that helped offset the loss I experienced.

As I started each phase of my career, I walked into it knowing that I had a lot to learn. I dove into learning what to do and listened to mentors, not just in insurance, but even before that as a shoe salesman.

> **I knew and still know that everyone and every situation has something to teach me.**

Lessons are not the only important thing. Knowledge is too. I consider myself a geek in whatever field I am working in. In insurance, I found all the small and large details fascinating. I loved to "talk" insurance. I would read anything I could get my hands on. And I attended any conference or learning opportunity and eventually started speaking at many of them.

As I ventured into self-storage, I subscribed to every self-storage magazine, attended every conference, and listened to every podcast. I wanted to learn everything I could.

Without a doubt, I am sure that I bored my wife to death over the years with all of the insurance, and later, self-storage speak. Understanding that I don't know everything keeps me constantly learning and growing.

As I think and plan for the future, I admit that I don't know what will happen. This last decade has been historic for growth in the commercial market. But change is most likely coming. I am so thankful to have a thriving business, a close family, and a community that encourages me.

Having Faith in the Bigger Picture

One of the lessons that has taken me years to learn is about the importance of trying to see the bigger picture through hard transitions and closed doors.

While in the midst of going through my hard work transitions, I struggled with what was happening. I felt betrayed and worried about how I was going to provide for my family. Some of the fear about being in poverty surfaced as well. However, looking back at every job I got and lost, every transition where the future was unknown, and every closed door, I saw that God was leading me through it.

The two biggest closed doors for me were Blue Shield and Johnson and Higgins. When I got hired by Blue Shield, I loved the environment and what I was doing. If advancement opportunities came, I saw myself working there for the rest of my career. The ending of that was hard.

Harder still was ending my job with Johnson and Higgins. I had poured my heart and soul into that company and genuinely loved working there. I had planned on staying with them until retirement.

Each of those endings was the beginning of something better. I didn't know it at the time, but if I had fought to stay or make it work, I would have missed out on what God had next for me. Even selling Western Benefit Solutions was the end of a dream and the beginning of a much larger dream.

I really try and encourage young people with my story. I want them to not get lost in the discouragement of closed doors, but keep looking for what is about to begin. Knowing that God has a plan for me and my family (and them and their family) is how we have faith in the bigger picture in our lives.

Blessings

Having a perspective to understand your blessings is all about gratitude. Thankfulness changes you.

I am thankful for the love and care I got from my mom growing up. I am so grateful for every opportunity I have had over the years—even the closed doors and missed opportunities.

My wife has also been a huge blessing to me. She is smart, funny, wise, and loving. She has been my rock and I would not be the man I am today without her. AJ, Alivia, Trevor, and Taylor are joys in my life and as they marry and add beautiful grandkids to the family, I am more and more blessed.

Every one of the employees I have, I am grateful for as well. They contribute skills and expertise to the business, but they also bless me personally. We are a family. When they struggle, I feel it. When they feel blessed, I feel that too. Our businesses grow and strengthen because of them.

Lastly, my church and friend communities bless me.

> **When we feel blessed and respond with gratitude, we bless others. It is one of those cycles that keeps giving and receiving.**

The Last Few Years

When AJ returned to work, he came with vision and passion. He also had a new perspective and wanted to make a difference in his sphere of influence—the self-storage community. I was grateful to not just have my son back to himself physically, but to have him and his passion in the office once again.

We really dove in headfirst into looking and acquiring self-storage facilities. Over the next few years, we bought larger and larger facilities. We also kept needing to expand our team and also needed to start other types of businesses to cover aspects of the business that weren't covered under Bitterroot Holdings.

We started Cedar Creek Wealth to facilitate investors who are interested in investing with us in storage facilities. Through Cedar Creek, we invest in and manage many self-storage facilities.

We are not just in the Pacific Northwest. We are even now expanding East as we find self-storage properties that fit our criteria. Our team at work continues to grow and the team at home continues to grow. Life is amazing.

As I look ahead to the future, I ask myself, where is the limit? Will I need to pivot? What new career or path is ahead? I may be hitting retirement age soon, but doesn't that just mean I will put on new "tires" and keep rolling? I am excited for the future.

CONCLUSION

Everyone comes from a different background. Some people are given everything and it's up to them to figure out what to do with it. Other people have nothing, not even a home or single family member. The rest of us fall in between. I came from extreme poverty and had to overcome many things, but there are others who have had harder beginnings.

No matter where you have come from, if you have given in to the hardships and challenges and allowed them to break you, you can still make a different choice. You can choose a different path . . . for yourself and your children.

I chose a different path as soon as I could make the choice for myself. I chose differently and I thought differently. I didn't want to raise my kids in poverty. I wanted to break that mentality of lacking finances, family structure, and a purpose-filled life.

As I look back over my life, there are simple life and business truths that helped break the poverty mentality of my family and community.

Know who you aren't. Know who you don't want to be. Look at the people around you and know that you will be the average of them. If they are not who you want to be, find people who are. You are not a failure, even if you occasionally fail. Make choices about who you *do* want to be. Even now—at whatever age you are—you can choose who you don't want to be.

You don't have to become your past. Were you raised with a poverty mentality? Be generous. Were you raised in addiction? Choose balance and health. Were you raised with mental health issues? Change your lifestyle and seek help. Make different choices. You not only don't have to become your past, but you definitely don't have to raise your children or run your business with that mentality.

Don't be afraid to try something different from everyone around you. This is how you will break the mindset that you were raised in. It is about making different choices, walking a different path, and thinking different thoughts. Your mindset is truly in your mind. And thinking differently leads to doing different things.

> **"To rise out of poverty you must change your way of thinking. You can't live in abundance with impoverished thoughts."**
> **—Germany Kent**

Be intentional with your family. Be intentional with your business, friends, and yourself. Chose the right things. Make choices that lead to a healthy lifestyle not just physically, but mentally and emotionally as well. The healthier you are, the more you will get out of life.

Relationships are the key to business and a meaningful life. Develop your relationships with clients, coworkers, employees, and other business owners. Everybody is unique and has something to offer. Be genuinely interested in them. People attract similar types of people, so if you are caring and generous, you will most likely attract caring and generous people. But if they try and take advantage of you, have boundaries and don't be afraid to walk away. Not everyone has your best interest at heart.

Be content and don't always say no, but mostly say no. If you are always looking for the next thing, you may miss what you have. On the other hand, if you always say no, you may miss opportunities that come your way. Life is about balance.

Do what is best for the client. When you meet your client's needs, they stay (or return). We all know that the customer is *not* always right. And it is not about that. To establish loyal customers, they need to know that you can and will help them meet their needs.

Hold on in the tough times. They will come and they will go but if you can hang on, things improve. Hardships work to teach us and if we can learn from them, we become better people. We also find out who we can rely on, and that strengthens our relationships.

Have perspective about growth and blessings. Stop and smell the roses. And when you have done that, look at where you started, what you went through and overcame, and where you are now. It is important to also think about the future, your goals, and what might come. Having a grateful perspective changes you. Be grateful about where you came from and who and what you have now.

You can do it. You can break an unhealthy mindset for you and for your family. Making good, different choices changed my life and it will change yours.

CHAPTER 1 NOTES

CHAPTER 2 NOTES

CHAPTER 3 NOTES

CHAPTER 4 NOTES

CHAPTER 5 NOTES

CHAPTER 6 NOTES

CHAPTER 7 NOTES

CHAPTER 8 NOTES

CHAPTER 9 NOTES

OVERALL BOOK NOTES

ACKNOWLEDGMENTS

There are so many people I would like to thank. I am who I am because of the family, friends, mentors, bosses, employees, and leaders I have had in my long—but not yet done—life. Much of this book (and my life story) is about relationships.

First and foremost, I want to thank my wife, Carla. You have been my constant companion, support, partner, and adventure-buddy on this ride we call life. Thank you for pouring your life and love into our kids and grandkids. Thank you for helping grow them into the adults they are or will be.

Thank you to AJ, my firstborn. Your vision and tenacity with your family, work, and life are something to be proud of. Tessa, you make AJ a better man and are an amazing mom, entrepreneur, and teacher.

To my favorite daughter, Alivia. I am so proud of you for who you are. You are pouring your life into your kids, pursuing your dreams, and making a difference to those around you. Sam, thank you for bringing a different and much needed perspective to our family and company while being a loving father and faithful husband. Don't tell anyone, but you are definitely my favorite son-in-law.

Trevor, thank you for bringing not just humor and laughter into this family, but also insight, wisdom, adventure. You liven every conversation you are a part of but also drop nuggets of truth and understanding. Amy, you are smart, hardworking, personable, and a veritable angel, especially to our family.

Thank you, Taylor, first and foremost for being who you are. You are caring and supportive to not just me, but also your mom and siblings. Thank you also for being willing to serve as an officer in the United States Army. You are making a difference in this world.

To my incredible grandkids. You enrich my life with your different personalities and strengths. I am so excited to see who you all grow up to be.

Mom, thank you for pouring your life into me and my siblings, working so hard to keep food on the table and a roof over our heads, and for loving us even when it was hard.

To my in-laws, thank you for taking me into your family and accepting me as your own. Your example of love, devotion, hard work, and determination has made a difference in my life.

To the mentors who have changed me: Thank you for encouraging me, building me up, and showing me how to thrive in life. I will be forever grateful to you.

And finally to my intrepid writing and publishing team at Aloha Publishing: Heather, you took my stories and lessons and

ACKNOWLEDGMENTS

made them interesting and readable. Maryanna, thank you for having vision for this book and for the one(s) to come. And to the rest of the Aloha Publishing team, thank you for all the hard work that went into making this book look stunning, sound amazing, and for the care you took merging my story with the important principles that would inspire and challenge others.

ABOUT THE AUTHOR

Ron Osborne is the founder and CEO of Bitterroot Holdings, and president of Cedar Creek Wealth, both based in Eagle, Idaho.

Ron was born into extreme poverty. As a child, he learned the importance of relationships early, and he actively sought role models and people he could learn from to be part of his life. Not wanting to be held back by the mindset of his family and local community, Ron spent years learning how to change his thoughts and actions so that he, his kids, and his grandkids could lead a different life. He wanted them to understand the possibilities that come from living a life of generosity, hard work, and freedom.

Ron spent years working in the insurance industry, both for corporations as well as for himself, before diving into the self-storage business with his oldest son, AJ, and son-in-law, Sam. Ron co-founded Western Benefit Solutions, an insurance brokerage, in 1997 and grew it into a successful employee benefit brokerage firm based in Idaho with clients all around the United States. He sold the company to an international insurance brokerage firm in 2012. That same year he founded Bitterroot Holdings, focusing almost exclusively on self-storage commercial real estate, which he had been involved with since 2005.

Ron currently lives in Meridian, Idaho, with his beautiful wife, Carla, and eight extraordinary horses. They have four amazing adult children, two daughters-in-law, one son-in-law, and six adorable grandchildren (though they are hoping for at least a dozen more).

CPSIA information can be obtained
at www.ICGtesting.com
Printed in the USA
BVHW050523290822
645565BV00001B/61

9 781612 062716